SO-AAK-665

The Clear Blue
Lobster-Water Country

ALSO BY LEO CONNELLAN

The

Clear

Blue

A Trilogy

by

Leo Connellan

Lobster-Water Country

HARCOURT BRACE JOVANOVICH, PUBLISHERS

San Diego New York London

Copyright © 1985, 1983, 1981 by Leo Connellan
Foreword copyright © 1985 by Harcourt Brace Jovanovich, Inc.
All rights reserved. No part of this publication may be
reproduced or transmitted in any form or by any means,
electronic or mechanical, including photocopy, recording,
or any information storage and retrieval system, without
permission in writing from the publisher.

Requests for permission to make copies of any part of the
work should be mailed to: Permissions, Harcourt Brace
Jovanovich, Publishers, Orlando, FL 32887.

Any resemblance between characters here portrayed
and persons living or dead is purely coincidental.

Library of Congress Cataloging in Publication Data
Connellan, Leo.
    The clear blue lobster-water country.
    I. Title.
PS3553.O5114C5   1985   811'.54   84-12955
ISBN 0-15-118135-7
ISBN 0-15-618054-5 (pbk.)

Designed by Dalia Hartman

Printed in the United States of America

First edition

A B C D E

This trilogy is for
Ida Elizabeth Carey Connellan,
who was my mother.

Contents

In Books I and II, stanza breaks between pages are indicated by a _____.

Foreword

We are late into the American Century, and by now most of our poets have associated themselves with colleges and universities. Whether this development signals, as some suggest, a decadence in our literary culture is a difficult question. One thing is surely unmistakable, however: The author of this trilogy is in this matter, as in many, exceptional. He has for years operated not only without academic tenure but also without any institutional ratification of his right to *be* a writer.

Leo Connellan's only "tenure," in fact, has been his fierce inner conviction that patience, courage, and honesty must result in the only poetry worth its name, and by corollary that language manipulated to please one's "superiors" is necessarily twisted into something worse than failure. Such language—oddly shared by truly academic writers and such memorable Connellan characters as Bludgeon and Featherhat—lapses into amorality.

How tempting it must have been for Connellan—in a life so harrowingly difficult that it would be pretentious for a middle-class poet like me to anatomize it—to sink precisely into such self-serving cynicism. This poet's palpable gifts (the lyric facility, the yen for narrative, the brilliant eye) could easily have enabled him to flatter fashion. Yet in the trilogy *The Clear Blue Lobster-Water Country*, more even than in his excellent and undernoticed preceding collections, Connellan has dared to fit the self-description of his persona, Boppledock. Bop asserts: "I am a victim of belief. / I recover and go on until my work is done / or my last breath is snuffed. . . ."

In what sense a victim? We can think of Bop's faith in love-as-reconciliation, a faith that brings with it the refrain of heartbreak: "Father, we'll / meet again. / You can tell me you love me then." Or, perhaps more pertinently, we can note Bop's claim that "purity of motive is harder to achieve / than the hardest betrayal. . . ." In short, it is the stunning integrity of Connellan as writer and man that has been so costly.

Yet the poet's almost incredible struggle to keep the purity of his motives alive amid the welter of fraud and deception around him also leads to a kind of redemption. "I am put together again hard," says Bop in the final movement. "I will break / no further, I have become me."

Not that Connellan would claim, through his persona, that he is virtue embodied. If *The Clear Blue Lobster-Water Country* were no more that a victim's testimony, if it were simply a grand "J'accuse" directed at American society—a genre fashionable enough among many poets who have a good deal less reason than this one to mount an attack—it would lack the power implicit in Bop's affirmation. But if, as Bop also avers, "Cure lies in us," it follows that our spiritual and bodily illness also lies in us. Connellan's belief in the accuracy of testimony demands that he scrutinize not just the darker side of American life, but his own self-betrayals as well. By holding to an achingly candid poetry—devoid of posture, composed in isolation, and without external reward, yet founded on human love—Connellan has certified the importance of his own voice.

It is a voice like no other in current poetry in America. Surely its form(s) and diction(s) will raise the eyebrows of the genteel. Surely many conventional critics and scholars will dismiss as eccentric the poet's views—or more aptly visions—of Irving, Dickinson, Crane (and behind them all, Whitman), and other native luminaries. It is precisely, however, Connellan's dual capacity to speak the sprawling, raucous American idiom and to understand the national literary tradition *from within* that has resulted in his uniqueness now.

I will probably persuade no reader of classical bent to relish *The Clear Blue Lobster-Water Country*. It is a book intended for everybody—perhaps most especially for those who do not normally read what passes for poetry among us—but some will refuse its invitation. But I firmly believe that readers who esteem those works of American literature that strive against powerful odds to see to the heart of what an artist is—a striving so integrally and frequently connected with the effort to understand that great thing, "America"—will value this abrasive and annoying and perspicuous and ultimately lovely mass of verse. They will honor Leo Connellan for having *persisted*, for remaining sturdy (one thinks of Melville here) in debilitating circumstance. They will applaud his determination to find the democratic virtues of decency, compassion, charity, and straightforwardness. For those same virtues are the very premises of the belief that has victimized this poet, but of which, as this trilogy amply shows, he has also been the final beneficiary. And we, too, thanks to his labor of generosity.

SYDNEY LEA
September 1984

Acknowledgments

I would like to thank Alexander Harvey of
Hollow Spring Press, who published Book One
and Book Two of this trilogy in small press
editions, and the Connecticut Commission on the
Arts for an Individual Artist's grant, which
aided the writing of the lyric narrative
"Shatterhouse," Book Two of this trilogy.

Book One:

Coming to

Cummington

to Take

Kelly

I

Father, we'll
meet again.

You can tell me you love me then.

I went to your Rice Paddy when
you gave me choice between prison,
running, or places I
had no right being, but
I love you, Father, love you.
It's a hot love. I wish
you loved me too.

You'd send me anyplace!
I need your love enough to go.
I stand unemployed now bewildered.
People look at me like
I'm something awful!

I'll show them! Father, help
me, I seek you, the
original dream.

I'll fight for your love!
Look what I do
for you.

Come to Cummington
to take Kelly.

Not Wilbur he's
True and Great . . . nor Herman Melville either . . .

   . . . take a good look
at Port Hill Road, yes, it's
likely Kelly runs it, better face
facts, when you're taking a man on
you can get killed. He didn't
come for you,
you came for him . . .

Washington Irving, hold your
myth in that painting congealed.
Do not let them out again, that
crew, not yet, no
not for a while yet . . .

For you, Father, I
imagined up a contest.
Sought out an adversary
where none exists,
to win your heart beyond
the grave where I
never had it here.

We'll meet again and you
can tell me you love me then.

. . . Will my only child, daughter,
seek me out as I seek you out!?

II

It is the nature of predatory
stalkers, failing to corner pleasure,
to slide into catastrophe, now,
of sexual monogamy, except
when she wants to have a fling;

and, thinking she failed me,
as I am come to feel I failed
you, Father, seek me out as I
seek you.

She is me in reverse, Father.
Young woman stalks the male now, she's
got the box to put it in and can
give a coronary of ego.

But she knows that my love
was hers . . . is hers . . . Father,
here I am as now age crowds
my youth out of sight . . . No one
in the world will see me
young anymore . . . only
my dreams are young.
And my lust is young.

Father, my child never has to wonder
if I love her, here it is
even written for her to see
when like the dry brown leaf
I am crumbled and gone.

My love is my wife's too, but she
was abandoned in your demand of me
and is full of disgust, annoyance
at the very mention of you. It is
my need to seek you, Father, she
is revolted by what you are, what
we, you and I were together
in Rice Paddies, as we were too
long ago in the trade of flesh.
. . . signing our Declaration of

Independence, calling ourselves
"land of the free" at
auctions of human beings.

For you, Father, I
come to Cummington
to take Kelly.

You did not know me
on this earth, Father,
resented to know me,

guilt full, guilt driven.
Violated, the child's
mother died when he
was seven and told she'd
gone to take care of a
little boy who needed
her more than he did . . .

Father, this while
you hung away from home
sniffing your lost opportunities
on the bum.

III

We come to Cummington
to take Kelly.

Should we really go
to Wellesley . . . ?

Is this "Kelly"
the "Kelly" we want . . . see

how it goes, Father, in my
invention . . . Coming To Cummington
To Take Kelly, a short folk song,
no, a cantilena by
El Bardo The Legend, your son.
Father, it will be easy enough
to concoct . . . Let's "Play Something!"
"Make Believe" . . . remember?
You sent us boys to Summer Camp
where my brother was
at home as moths in linen, but
I was despondent and lonely.

It was no place for me.
You did not know that
and meant only generosity
sending me too where
you sent the son you loved.

And in a crowd of bunk
rope cutters, Canoe
Paddle thieves I had to
keep my mouth shut and
not tell on them although
no one took me in their group
for keeping my mouth shut.

And punishment wasn't
a Counselor's touching you,
no, the grown men were too smart.
You don't whack paying customers
unless you catch them picking pockets
or something, you get a boy
to discipline boys. His name
was Kelly. It was horror.

I was wheat cut down by a scythe
I never did anything to, hit
and splattered fat lip, Father,
I can imagine him up for us, I will!

Wilbur, forgive my borrowing
Cummington.

Poverty allows few arenas.
My time is running out.

Still, my own imagination
must run its risk! Yet, it
would be treachery to tread
on Providence, Rhode Island,
Poe footprints, or
accost Emily Dickinson, to
combat someone in front of
her atrocity! . . . to try
to rescue Anthony Hecht's King
headed for flaying
would necessitate
going back into a
time I know nothing about,
better to fail trying
something I comprehend or
to win because I do.

"The strange man of the
mountain, his clothing of Dutch
fashion," has come for me.

"Figures in an old
Flemish painting that hung
in the parlor of Dominie

Van Shaick" come
for me now.

IV

Father, here is my scheme!
In "Running" by Wilbur,
Poem 11 'PATRIOT'S DAY
          (Wellesley, Massachusetts ,'
last stanza, page 27, in
"Walking to Sleep," lines 13 to 16,
clearly, Poet has taken his
little son to see little children run
of whom he says that one,
(which one!?) is . . . "our"
Kelley as big people have
Boston Marathon John Kelley . . . then
why stretch logic
even for you, Father,
to pick a fight go like
a sorehead bulbous nose
out of joint malcontent
to make trouble in serenity!?
Because the draw rope
on my well
is broken.

And with your horse
shot from under you
death coming from
all sides now, briefly,
fleetingly, you recall
with great welling of
anguish the places you
wanted to get to in

order to fix the rope
and bring up your dream again.

But standing in
dusty alone you die
as best you can absolutely
no good at it, with style
and a flair if this is
your last song you try then
to change your character
to be what the appalling
situation seems to require
that after a lifetime
against taking life you now
try to kill them well
so those who are left
will ride off, they won't
mutilate you, but will
look with honor on you
dead in the middle of their dead
. . . hoping a minstrel will come by
and see the great tapestry
of you and them and go
sing down the roads
of "El Bardo The Legend," "Lahty" . . .
. . . See what I mean, Father?
What silliness can be
thought up to capture
your heart.

But I have a simple plan
to run and box a man
to win your love
beyond the grave.

———

We'll meet again.
You can tell me you love me then.

One thing too, Father, there
will be no Roncesvals Gaston treachery
in this cantilena . . . nothing like
what happened to Roland! . . . It will be clean.
Truly dedicated too, to you, Father,
for you, Father, but dedicated to
Gauffridi of Aix and Giordano Bruno
burned at the stake, God forgive us!
For you, Father, dedicated to them.

V

Now, Father . . . of all the
Kellys in the world why
go way up into the Berkshires
after one!?

Because it is high up there
and you have to go there
out of your way. I want you to
see me, Father, going out of
my way to do battle and
let's see what happens!

Father we'll "Play Something!"
Remember? . . . When I was a
little boy I'd walk along
talking to myself "Playing Something."
I'd come out of a movie slouched
with a cigarette hanging
from my Alan Ladd lip. I was

Graham Greene's James Raven
with the deformed wrist.

Now, Father, you and I will
do it again . . .

Look what I do for you!

This fat little gray man
with the potbelly snout
is Lahty!

Remember your "Lahty" singing
"Home on the Range" at age five
strumming on a cigar box banjo, remember
your "Boppledock!?"

Daddy do you remember your "Boppledock!"
. . . There wherever you are . . .

You just fell down
in front of a garage, the
cold stained concrete
grease like black blood
was your bed when you
hit that great bald head to death.

You were gone
and I didn't
have you anymore.

There wherever you are do
you ever think of Boppledock
with fat squirrel pouches Apple cheeks?

———

When they found you dead
the photograph of me
in your wallet was a
seven-year-old-boy photograph.

The photograph of my brother
was of him as a grown man.

VI

My brother and I never
had a chance to
like each other the
way we grew up was
each one for himself.

Full of hurt, heartbreak,
you screaming, "I
must be appeased!"

You screaming, Daddy!
Why, you were so
frustrated you used to
chew handkerchiefs
red in the face.

You'd pull a handkerchief
out of your pocket just
as you were about to scream
and bite down on it hard
like a man having his arm
cut off without anesthesia.

I think I know now
you were hustled

out of your dreams
before you ever
had them.

Your life was
disappointed in guilt
from birth to hesitate, to
scream at everyone like
anyone suddenly grabbed
and held and branded
not only white-hot on flesh
but deep within.

You screamed not ever
realizing why you
cried out which was
because yourself was
stolen from yourself
by Irish church and your
own ruined branded parents
bringing you up blessing yourself
in an age when to dare realize it
was beyond society's cope. So you
lived a wasted man, ruined
potential, you laid
on us, my brother
Young Billy and me as
it had been driven
into you like the
spikes in Christ's palms.

Your genius snuffed out,
I write it for you, Father,
because you are dead
and cannot ever now

have it all dawn on you
and write it for yourself, it
is a statement I make for you
because you can no longer.
A job I finish for you
only because I lived
long enough to and
love you.

We'll meet again.
You can tell me you love me then.

My love for you
overcomes memory, my
love of you, Father,
blots out the
horror of your screams
on the heart and joy
of my childhood your
screams like snakes of needles
aimed at inside my head
to somehow burn out
my reason, to smother
natural intuition,
comphehension . . . the
job got almost done
as it did with you.
But it wasn't accomplished
and this is my song to us
song of El Bardo The Legend
to his Father, to the world.

. . . In America, Washington Irving,
you have to be a peddler
of your wares, you can be

the great poet but only known
for smoking Pot, as something
funny running up and down
college corridors chasing
a boy not for poems!
We play to causes and audiences,
make sure we make everyone
feel superior, we're less
than they are, they don't
come up to us, we come down
to them or miss success is
where art is in America, Washington
Irving . . . where is your
fantasy gone, your spell
woven for us along
the Tappan Zee, up
in the woods of the Hudson?

. . . Father, we've got to
get this out of the way, was it
a mistake you made I
constantly reminded you of,
something you lost
I reminded you of . . .

> . . . It was always whispered
> you were engaged to marry
> Mother's sister who
> took you her catch up to the
> annual family Christmas sing-
> around-the-piano where the
> family stentorian loud phonies
> burst forth in song as
> though something had been

waiting all year to hear them
and you "saw" Mother and
that was "it!" No one ever
explained how you dropped
Aunt Cynthia. I knew her a
long time, into my middle age,
she looked relieved to
have me her nephew, pronounced "Neview."

. . . Did you, Smilin' Billy, sin!?
Naw, not you! C'mon! If
you did I like you, if you did
you put me in good company.

You wouldn't take Mother away
from singin' round piano
would you . . . not you!

Was it hard
to take bringing me up?

No? Tell me no, then,
when we meet
tell me.

What soap opera! The show
apparently is "El Bardo The Legend And Fa"
or "Lahty And Father" on
two every afternoon
with my tears lost in TV sets.

Who can find the true American broken heart
in the Diarrhea Commercial.

———

My only brother and I
never had a chance
to ever like each other.

There is cruelty between us.
Young Billy's self-protective
defense is criticism.

My brother Billy is
full of advice. It's
the dirty cracks that
are hard to forgive.
All the lousy remarks
he felt there'd never be
a way in the world he'd
regret saying anything
he felt like.

He felt violated, afraid
I'd sponge off him,
rob him. He was robbed
of his only mother too
at only six and screamed at
by his idol Smilin' Billy
all his childhood forced
to feel filthy, guilty
about erections, girls,
getting horny, rushed
to Confessional in the
church that was always
changed after burdening
mankind with dictates, as
it suits itself, daring to
tell us we'll never "see God's
face!" Father preaches down at

the Methodist church now and
over at the Synagogue . . . so,
God, I'll see you sometime. I
"see" you right now that you
forgive me because I am sorry,
because I want to come to you.
. . . My only brother had to run
for himself, to save himself, rush
for his own life from horror.
Thank God he did it.

Father, I have to say it,
this is between us, you
and old Boppledock . . . my
brother and I never
had a chance to be close.

We were robbed of
our mother and
cheated of each other.

We are the children
of violation.

"I must be appeased!"
You'd scream, Big Billy!
You'd stop your Chevy
right in the middle
of Main Street, didn't
matter, traffic would
be backed up, little
boys' nervous systems
never mattered.
"I must be appeased!"

———

You could be drooling
and see some middle-aged
baseball bat swinger
come along who once
hit one over the fence
and how you could
turn it off, the screaming
at us boys and turn on
charm becoming "Smilin' Billy"
discussing next night's
game and plays and the
second he left, an
hour later, an
hour later!, turn red
face screaming
"I must be appeased!" back on.

As grown men my
brother and I hardly
see each other . . . Father,
look what I do now,
imagine this whole
short folk song, work
it all out with a villain
I must go conquer like
one of your basketball
contests of nonexistent enemies
shooting balls through holes of string
to raving cheers forgotten
as soon as there was a new tournament.

VII

We come to Cummington
to take Kelly.

———

I who ran against
Buck Shot and won.

Is this "Kelley"
the "Kelly" we want?

See, Father, got to
work it out think of
everything . . . like
. . . After searching phone book years
and, physically, always Irish,
many Kellys, never "the" Kelly.
In "Running" by Wilbur, line
"who would win again"
drew our eyes to who
would win again, "Kelley,"
triggered odd hostile
resentment in us,
all fixes lived through . . . see,
Father, how this develops!
. . . The stanza could sound
like races prearranged
so all others are going
through running motions
surrounding Kelley, who,
in among them will win
again, rather than
what it was, a
cocky, confident champion
sure in himself he
would take anyone running
with him that day, his
danger would be not to
really run and so be

upset by Joe the
Garbage Man's son . . . is this
what we have here . . . Father!?
Really!? . . . Isn't Wilbur's
poem simply and only about
little children . . . How far
do I go for you, Dad!?

. . . The danger, Father, is
attributing ability to
children, in other words, insanity.
Exercising paranoia . . . see how far
I'll go for your love . . . went to
Rice Paddies . . . we'll
meet again beyond the grave,
you can tell me you love me then.

VIII

We come to Cummington
to take Kelly.

I who ran against
Buck Shot and won.

Could "Kelly" be
in Cummington?

Or is my Kelly boyhood
Summer Camp Counselor
bully of frightened youth
really now some Kelly of
South Boston's Breed's Hill,
beery faced with blank
little wormy eyes with

murdering busing blacks in them?
Embarrassingly, we
aren't having any
luck finding the Kelly
we want, a Kelly who
has vanished among Kellys . . . or
now we're grown up and, as
his victim, he's important
to us but he always eluded us
by never hiding because he
doesn't think he did
anything to hide from,
so in this irony
he is vanished.

I am looking for
a "Kelly" and believe
he's put an *e*
after the last *l* in
the name "Kelly" before
the *y* and is in
Cummington . . .

He was solid, stalky, freckled,
conceited and had never been hurt so
he enjoyed hitting.

Frightening thing was
that he really was good and
beat opponents his own
age and weight with blood
lust of joy in it.

Summer Camp Counselors
were afraid of him too and

fed him small boys to
hit, they'd make you
get in a boxing ring with
this Kelly and he'd expose
the coward out of you from
where you had fairly
well hid it. One day
you read Wilbur's
"Running," in Poem 11
a "Kelley" was in it
"content" within this
run . . . Sure he would
win again, as he
had always won . . . your cracking
skull seized on what you wanted
to be true, too full of
vengeance lust to think
clearly, that Wilbur
was "noting" that a "Kelley"
was content within this
run, not him, he, "Kelley"
wasn't saying he was content
within this run or that he
would win again, no, he said
none of this, but your
temple-pounding desire to
find him obliterated
your even observing the
double intention underneath
reference to the Kelleys
of Boston Marathon, wiped
out your ability to
even see the name of
this runner . . . "Kelley"
not "Kelly" . . . worse, your

insanity prevented your
realizing there is no one
in the "Running" poem by
Wilbur really named "Kelley"
or "Kelly" . . .

. . . See, Father, my
thoughts are become
like caramel syrup as I
"Make-believe try" to make
this work for you . . . but
all things are created out
of an adolescence, maturity
risks fearing to chance . . . I
would rather fail at this, Father,
and try, than grow old scared.

IX

We're in Cummington to
take Mr. Kelly . . . Kelley?
So well hidden in the
Berkshires where no one
ever knows where
anyone lives if you ask them.

But I come to Cummington
to take him. Come to me Kelly
or I'll come to you.

You run, they say, but
do you box!? The Kelly
I want, I come to
Cummington to take, boxed.

———

We can pitch a tent
while we run a couple of
days to know the roads
a little, although isn't
running running? Keep
your shoelaces tied
and don't trip.

We can stay in a tent in
Cummington or in a motel
down below Deerfield on
Old College Road if
Whale Inn's full.

It's easy to track
if you know a place but if
you've just plunged in
few will help you.

The Chief of the
Fire Department in
Cummington wouldn't
tell you where someone
lived, but anyone
will tell you where
a road is if you give
its name.

     . . . One day in Summer
     Camp in your violated
     indignation . . . how
     do you explain violation
     and to whom? . . . pain
     horror screams screaming
     into silence.

Like indignant unbroken
child slapping back, you tried
to beat up your own brother
in that Kelly ring, Saturday
night challenges to get in
good with Counselors, ingratiate
the camp . . . and you fixed it
so your brother couldn't
get out of getting into
the ring with you, the beating
fear of Kelly did that to you,
twice as big and two years older
than your brother . . .

You went for your little brother
who went for both your
thumbs in the gloves like
swollen noses, spraining
them both and then didn't
finish you.

No one ever took Kelly
who came from somewhere
around "Bawston" . . . is
Cummington where that
bastard Kelly is with a
fancy letter *e* faking
you out between the last *l*
and the letter *y*? . . . was
the Kelly you're after
a runner!? He was
a boxer . . . but was
he a runner!?

We've got to show him

we lived, survived,
grew up and have
lasted to run him down.

We're as big
as he is now.

X

We drive into Cummington
someone left out, child
whose father loved
his brother more than
he loved him, pulp of
flesh with goopy eyes in
an incubator, he hated you
for that and your mother
almost left him over it.

Now in your old youth
you still feel ache pang emptiness,
dry heaves of tears that
never come, they were
cried long ago. You
fantasize home again,
now the house jumps back
into your head, the
porch you crouched on
playing Cowboys and Indians;
the hallway from the
living room chair you
sat crouched in looking
at tree branches through
the side panel glass of
the front door slowly

waving, the wind in
them sound was like
your mother's dress
sounded to your little
ears in the middle of
mischief times you
heard her coming
down from upstairs, you
sat listening watching
those trees waiting for
your mother. She died
but they didn't tell you
that. They told you she'd
gone away to take care
of a little boy who needed
her more than you did and
you sat waiting for her to
finally finish with that
other boy and come back. Now
you see your father tossing
you out of the house onto
the porch when divvy
time came.

Now you drive 5–9 into
what imagination runs
crazy, yearning, fear
one is outside what
one's heart needs, one
is deprived so into the
serene luxury to be
taken in and embraced
at last by your father . . . you'll
find this Kelly and you'll
run and box him good to defeat . . .

And your father, Smilin' Billy,
will toss and catch apples
back and forth with you the
way he did with your brother,
wear a baseball cap cockeyed
visor turned to the side on his
head with you, the way he did
with your brother . . .
But the old man
is dead Rip Van Boobie!
Buried now under the tulips
of deciduous forever . . .

XI

Yet in a Nursing home you
gave up a couple of skid row
wine blasts to get him in
away from those awful ones
with squirrels running intimately
up the arm of Smilin' Billy now
he's got strokes, you sat with him
alone by his bed in the dark
hospital room and put your
hand in his hand and
he knew you were there, he
squeezed it and the
broken doll's moonbeam
face, silly in blood clot,
smiled as he squeezed
your hand getting strength
from it as if you were the bouncing
rubber ball he was depending on.
And when nurse came in
he said from beyond his

stabbed apathy . . .
"You see, I have two sons!"

XII

We come to Cummington
to take Kelly.

Take a good look at Port Hill
Road, yes, it's likely Kelly
runs it, his legs in the
thighs of the machine of
himself, two hard rubber balls
squeezing pistons, not
sponges, his wind exceptional for
his age, only the fact of years
inhibits him and don't count on
that, yes, he does run up Port Hill
Road to maple-shaded red house
on top left across just down from
Gates' white house, the road
levels there.

Kelly trains running
Fairground Road running
right, a rough run, the
workout road Kelly runs
on, up Dodwells Road past
red barn weeping willows up
into night black green, up!
The Martini heart
now knows quitting time.

Perhaps . . . is Kelly
Kelly poor boy running

to Master whims, perhaps
that's it! He's bullyboy to
get summers in camp for
himself, Patriot Day running
champion to be favorite and
so sponsored . . . "get Kelly (Kelley)
he'll run for you!" . . . like
animals who run Triple Derbies,
then are put out to procreate
stagger among the daisies
until they break something
and are shot.

We've got to race him,
to finally make it with Father
in hallucination it's all for
children his fists broke.

XIII

We'll park by the Fairgrounds,
come up every day dressed to
jog, not saying anything, just
doing it, just get out of the
car and run the roads to see
if we can make them
and we'll be in everybody's
eye, probably somebody's
relative or forgotten
son gone a long time, home
from somewhere, recalled
on the rim of minds as a
ten-year-old, if dwelt on,
we, someone who never

existed here, but mistaken
for someone who did because
people do not wish to think
a stranger could just drive
into Cummington, get out
of a car dressed like their
neighbor runner and run up
and down through their privacy,
mistaken for someone they
all know, if they just stop
and think on it.

So we've got to run . . . all
we want is to run, run
and rest! . . . and run
until we've run and run
against Kelly . . . like a
Lion loose here, where
the air is like cow shit through buttermilk.

XIV

. . . Kelly (Kelley) I have run
races alright, running from
cops clanging red freight car
door to beat eight months' automatic
on the road chain gang
outside Denver . . . can
you imagine so dumb
as to be headin' into
Denver not knowing the
Railroad Detective Training
School was there and my
Olympic possibilities for

our team, old buddy, were
proven when I leaped a
fence as a boy fast enough
with my pockets full of
somebody else's Crab Apples
to beat Buck Shot headed
for my ass. Buck Shot goes
like human runners too,
there's a shot and you're off,
but Buck Shot isn't human
and so doesn't have to
breathe right or pace,
it goes directly for
the finish line and if
you're running ahead of it
and it doesn't catch you,
you ought to be up for
invitation to run in
Cummington to try to take Kelly.

XV

. . . We are seen now, the
only way to get out of this
now, humiliation of being
beaten again, to call out
loudly for all to hear

        "Just foolin' " or
"sorry!" or, "Hey, Kel . . . Kelley?
I know you ran at Wellesley
long ago . . . but did you also
come down to Maine
to Summer Camp!?"

XVI

Kelly come down Dodwells Road
so fast his Flats slapped
the dusty earth held
back on itself.
A good-natured furrowed brow
over eyes so cold I could
see Nova Scotia in them.

He took a hard look at me
and I at him, no recognition,
for time shatters features
and attitudes, but
Kelly (Kelley) has the
heart of a Roman and the
survival instinct
of a running Christian.

I look at him hard . . . is
he the Kelly? Looked like
him because I wanted him to.
If he took the heart
out of me by not being
the Kelly, he had the race,
for I am one of those who
feel always cheated by
man and opportunity.

But Kelly run up Port Hill
Road, that road in Cummington
like it's a jumping out of a
Jack-in-the-Box snake, narrow
curving straight up, he went up
like he was drawn to the top, but

I could see for myself that
nothing was helping him.

I took off and in the
heat of my anticipation
that he'd win I
made the hill too, but
the gut of my running
was pulled to its belly button hook,
and one more step would unravel me.

There was Kelly on the
far side of Gates' house
trotting, fists driving exhausts.
You saw no flame
but the way they were closed,
I knew his hands had
grabbed all the
air they'd need to pull the
big sheet world to him, which
would look like running if
you didn't know what he
was doing.

He owned the earth of running, he
is Champion Kelley.

Then he ran right through me
as though a kite
had taken air.

XVII

And now, my Father, furious
at the spilt milk of me,

life is a blend of death that
didn't finish us. I have
imagined this up to win your
heart beyond the grave.

We'll meet again and you
can tell me you love me then . . .

. . . From an old Flemish painting
did that crew creep from the Portrait again
and, as they got old Rip . . . for twenty-five years
this time, got us sleeping again . . . giving
themselves new names for us to know them
by, Hudson, Nixon . . . and one of them
Joe McCarthy . . . There are always the
Dominie Van Shaicks to gave them such an
innocent place to hide as in a Portrait to
gaze down on us until we develop into
something to come out of hiding for . . . Washington
Irving, you told us where they were!

But, just where in Tarrytown . . . I know
the theories, but just where was
Van Shaick's house . . . we
must find the spot and turn it
into a national shrine of mourning, how
far from Sunnyside, Van Shaick's house!

. . . Now it's Kelly (Kelley) and
me on Cummington Berkshire
wide meadows for our ring
and the sawdust of dry
dusty road for our feet to
shuffle in as we closed and
moved to each other, me, with

the cold fear years thinking about
bad beating I took that hit
so hard at the virginity of
self-assurance as to almost
demolish it and make a life
for me of jumping every
time something clattered,
shaken, I ran scared
where God and my mother
intended I go bravely
into challenge with
endurance joy to struggle
to achieve instead of broken dread.

And now here to me came
he who hit so hard, but
the fatiguing destruction of
just surviving exhaustion
had long ago quashed my
initial fury and now here
came to me he who I had
come after in my head every
time weakness in me ruined
my pursuits, here was
some man named Kelly . . . was
he my Kelly? The anger that
furies vengeance at my
violation, which time lets
you enjoy as reason you
never risked much, so here we
stood now two old men and
me still not certain he is
"the" Kelly I want, here and
the heart of my fight gone

in the running he won winning
the lost happiness I was
looking for in taking him
and he saw it in my look
when we touched knuckles, yet,
still, the spineless animal
weakness to kill those
weaker than us, we think,
urged him to throw
his left at my nose now and
I hadn't thought he would so
didn't quite move out of the
way but was glazed along my
left eyebrow like splitting
plastic, a zipper opening,
then did I hit him with a
right I started at the
bottom of Mexico and delivered to him at the
top of the Alaska of his
jaw so he went down in Cummington,
but he had always loved the
take too, whereas I had not
liked any of it, so I
realized he had still won,
his happiness in surviving
blows as well as giving
them, nothing short of
killing him would win
for me and I wouldn't
do that and if I would
he'd be beyond feeling
what I did to him and in
the life of middle light
on the way to eternity,

outside of the flesh that
had been him, he'd look at
it, the body that had
carted him around, and at me
supposedly certain I'd
finally put an end to him,
and knowing eternal life,
would smile thinking of
my surprise on seeing him
again poised to run or
ready to throw blows
on the backside of the sun
where Mars' craters gape,
when it's my turn in the
long tunnel.

I turned to gaze on him to
see if I'd enjoy the earthly
sight of him lying on
Cummington ground, but before
I could consider whether I
would like seeing him down he
was up and jogging
and he was on flat Fairground
Road, then onto Dodwells and gone.

. . . Was he my Kelly?

Whole green
was absolutely quiet.

Like when thunder
has stopped clapping.

_____

Look what I did,
Father, look what I did
for you, come to
Cummington to take Kelly!

But there was a "Kelley"
Wilbur wrote of and
he took me . . . I cannot
go find what never existed . . . even
for us, Father!

Even for you and me, I am not
Warrior Knight or Athlete, but
I'm old Boppledock the apple-cheeked
kid you carried a picture of in your wallet . . .

And you, Hudson, back!
Back into your painting! I'm
wise to you and your booze.
My soul has been touched by you.
You have brushed my life
like windshield wipers separate
white snow, but the earth lust
of me still hates.

Not now, Hendrick, not quite yet!
Come into the woods with your sauce
another time. I will
drink you under table if I can
or you will put me to sleep then, but
I do not think you would let me wake again
to come out with what I know.

I don't commit the crimes you die for, the

crimes kill me. I am a victim of belief.
I recover and go on until my work is done
or my last breath is snuffed like
the palm of a hand on a candle.

Then, Father, we'll
meet again.

You can tell me you love me then.

Book Two:

Shatterhouse

I

Mother, we'll meet again.
I will tell you I love you then.

I went drinkin'
me, Bop, why not!

Drinkin' put me in
Little Hope Hospital.

Me, Bop, middle age now, become
like Stephen Crane characters,
"Mr. Blanc" and like the "Swede,"
almost insane in an alien environment
that does not understand him. Bop no
longer young, a furious Bop raging for
original America in fantasy Mace
and Armor seeking original American
virtue up in Cummington, Massachusetts to
do battle with and run against the great
Marathon Champion Kelley, really seeking

a boyhood Kelly tormentor . . . Now, my Mother,
America's become a nation of Peeping Toms
rather than participants. We seem to wish
to commit suicide, lost, imagination and
risk . . . lost risking, like Anthony Hecht
risking cruelty in classicism, the very
young French Legionnaire of
Hecht's "The Deodand"—where
has our Individualist like Jack London
gone, like Karl Shapiro poems, "Homo"
"Caitlin Thomas" . . . Karl Shapiro not

---

faculty at an Eastern College because
he stood up against Pontius Pilate's being rewarded.
. . . Almost to the end of your short life, Stephen
Crane, your whole reputation rested on manufactured
tales about things you knew absolutely nothing of,
which means you risked, took a chance, invested
yourself . . . before writing "The Men in the Storm," it
is said that you stayed up all night outdoors in a
snowstorm so that you could try to drench into
yourself through personal involvement, exposure, the
actual experience—not for really long enough to

really know what it's like to be out in the cold,
but nevertheless, we are told you did this, felt
it was necessary to experience before you wrote what
you now wanted to write . . . That was the old American!
. . . which taught you to become able, finally, to write
the greatest Western story ever written by anyone . . .
. . . Bop, thwarted, frustrated human being needing
identity, love, needing to be center of attention
who is at emotional point of needing to be
taken seriously by triggering circumstances
to become his own death, but needing someone

else, an executioner, to do it for us, drink, drugs . . .
. . . Bop very near to becoming like Stephen Crane's
Swede, finally pushing one person too many,
the gambler, gets what he most fears and yet
wants, his death—but Bop survivor discovers
it is up to us what happens. Cure lies in us.
. . . When you wrote "The Blue Hotel," Stephen
Crane, in the year you wrote it, it was startling
for probing and seeking into characters as you

dissected them, stunning, when you wrote, for a
creative writer to set a piece of writing

around a man obviously mentally ill and to show
what happened to him and the effect of it on
everyone—you were haunted all your brief life
by the dilemma every writer who is any good faces,
that of having to write about something in order
to learn to write at all, but on the other hand
constantly aware of not really knowing anything
worth telling . . . so one invests . . . one risks! . . . I
went drinkin' agin, me, Bop, why not!
Drinkin' put me in Little Hope Hospital . . .
'specially after me-n-Buffer Rose

discuss what happen to his daughter, Evelyn-n-
I don' recall it all clear 'til after
I'm outa what they call Detox-n-into "Th'Community"
in Little Hope, while Mrs. Bop's thinkin' I'm havin'
a breakdown . . . duzzis soun' like th'thoughts of
a man breakin' a'course not! . . . but everythin' is
overwhelmin'. Th'whole America I love-n-unnerstood
. . . I THOUGHT I unnerstood . . . is changed.
I hope it isn't gone . . . We get up every mornin'
-n-go look th'same t'th'physical eye
like a camera only takes the surface picture.

We went from the wheel to the moon,
underneath we are sunk in addiction . . .
. . . Mother, we ran and boxed a man
for Father, for true virtue, for ideals
expressed at America's inception . . . but
we cannot correct what exists by taking on
what does not. Cure lies in us.

. . . Mother . . . I been drinkin' agin . . . I
come upon a truth about great danger in America
now for your granddaughter, Lollibop . . . Mother,
Peer pressure to dissipate, self-destruct—but

that's not what set me drinkin . . . Mother,
I was a victim who gave up, not now, Mother, no
more, but I'm tellin' you 'bout when I went
drinkin' agin before I come to see it's in me
what I become and America again once more . . . Mother,
my Mother, we'll meet when the sun sits down
on the moon and all the geese fly nowhere and
all our breath is let go . . . I'll be meetin'
Father too an' who knows maybe even Young Billy,
my only brother is sorry we never had much
to do with each other as age's sudden wisdom

watching our own children's relating to each other,
realizing we often do what our spouses wish, rather
than what we sometimes ached to do, makes Young Billy
see as I do that long before women married us, neither
of us ever had a chance with each other, who knows—
maybe his adrenalin was the sustained hatred of me,
criticism of my very existence his life preserver . . .
. . . and to like me would have broken something in him;
the end of his anger his ruin—who knows
what he needed just to accomplish growing up, he'd lost
everything I had . . . too. Brothers are not

able to pick each other . . . should I have ever
yearned for anyone to ever count on after
you left me, Mother . . . Mother, Young Billy
and me never had a chance with each other . . . maybe
I'll see him again, too, though, Mother when
the lights get too bright for my eyes, Mother,

and I close them, my last hearing,
the sea of Maine in my dying ears . . . and ocean-cold
smell come suddenly to my nose . . . Look! Sea Gulls
in fog and the stink of the clam sea as
low tide takes me out . . .

II

Drinkin' again, I found myself in
Little Hope Hospital monitored by
Staff Lucy Bubblegum and Illys of
"The Community" like Bludgeon, Motorcycle
gang mentality here to help his trial and
Toothpick In Featherhat The Farter . . . The
Bop's turned from patient payphone in the
hall as Bop saw Lucy Bubblegum stepping
out of Staff room and in a low well
controlled functioning-in-society able
tone, Bop asked—"What would the proper

procedure be to request to be excused from a
Group Therapy session, not frequently, or even
twice, just once if a particular long-distance
call from New York City comes for me?" "Concerning
what!?" She chewed her gum, blank expressionless
face, cruel eyes taunting, hoping they
could cause something . . . agitate ill people off
balance, unable to fight her, her victims . . .
"Concerning what!" Mrs. Bop exploded . . . "You
mean this man is expected to tell you our
personal business!?" Bop waved his hand

to try to silence Mrs. Bop, show functioning-
in-society not getting shook by Lucy Bubblegum
since he had to stay there in Little Hope

after Mrs. left unless he signed himself
out against medical advice which wouldn't be
demonstrating how much he really wanted to
become well, and now he was beginning now to
fear. (It's too womb-warm here, warm beds
and good meals, "Staff" like aunts and Bop'd
actually been voted by fellow Illys six
"steps" his first try when he read his soul

out to them, to Bludgeon, George, Toothpick
In Featherhat The Farter, Lucy Bubblegum off
"The Orange Contract" six steps which meant
he was back on earth again among those who
could cast a vote) this wife-strife wife
tirade might cause his reevaluation . . . wife'd
leave Little Hope for real world of innocent
until proven guilty, personal privacy . . . no
need to tell anyone your personal business . . .
. . . Suddenly Boppledock's head felt like a
branding iron white-hot was cooking his skull,

it "hurt" . . . This "occurrence" could get me
reevaluated. I'd be brought up at Community
Meeting the best way being me doing it to me to
demonstrate to the Community I was aware that
in a social situation anger flared . . . Bop said
to Lucy Bubblegum who wasn't a nurse or
even a trained Psychologist, but held
his life in her grimace . . . "A man wants
to send us money to feed our child, pay
our rent while I'm in here benefiting from
all this yet unable to try to function in

society and he doesn't know how we do

things here at Little Hope Hospital, so,
to him, what his concern is liable to be
is that he's running a long-distance phone
bill from New York City and now how we do
things here at Little Hope to help people
that help has never helped before, time after
time, Little Hope after Detox Center, isn't
even known to our dear, dear friend who is
telephoning us from New York City to try to
be of help to us if he can, so, please,

Lucy (it was alright to use Staff's first
names, they encourage it and they use yours)
can you tell us the proper procedure to
request that if a long-distance telephone
call comes for me I'll be allowed to leave
whatever Therapy Group I'm in and take the
call . . . ?" Looking blank, her eyes barely
making their threat, Lucy Bubblegum said,
almost reverting to her 7th grade
self, blowing a bubble around her chew,
"I don't think that's important enough

to leave Group." (Was she just saying
this to see how me Bop'd cope with it and
in a social situation too . . . there right
in front of Bop's wife!?) "WHAT!" screamed
free wife . . . Heads of Desk Staff jerked
as one, yearning for Mrs. Bop . . . at
that moment the Barracudas would have
tossed Bop loose for her. Right there Bop
felt his control slip through his forehead.
The branding iron hot in his skull . . . "Is
there a doctor here!?" Bop heard from far

———

away . . . Mrs. Bop seemed saying
it. "This man, my Bop, Boppledock's
having a breakdown right here in
front of my eyes . . . " . . . Bop floating
. . . wondering—is that what they do
here at Little Hope, break you like
breaking a bone to then set it
right so it will heal right . . . is
that it . . . they want you to break
so you'll recognize yourself? . . .
. . . hey waidaminute!—(through

Bop's thinking—) I'm not crackin' she's
wrong! My Mrs.'s wrong! I'm thinkin' this
out here, duz that sound like th'thoughts
-of-aman breakin'!? . . . Here-m-I thinkin'
this out while Mrs.'s callin' f'doctors . . . I'm
not breakin' but it's a wonder I'm not.
—What worryin' him flooding in him now—
what a man of his generation could never
let himself come out with at his age in
therapy . . . The drinker overwhelmed with
conceiving . . . Drinkin' with Buffer Rose,

within that Guinness Stout-n-ice-cold ale . . . I Bop
come upon a truth . . . vague like flushing and
the voices far off when you've been knocked out,
like someone's over you sayin' "He's had enough!"
. . . Mrs. Bop standin' there yellin' f'help for him
-n-that he was havin' a breakdown while through Bop
the death you die while you're alive . . . I come upon a
truth, Buffer talkin', talkin' with Buffer Rose inna bar
we come into outa his car-n-it was my "shout" too,

but Buffer alright, he buys! We're
talkin'-n-suddenly what we're sayin'

is about th'great danger of these times
my little Lollibop lives in . . . Lollibop
-m-only child, her girlfriend, Evelyn,
Buffer Rose's daughter only 13 on Cocaine,
drink . . . They've put her every place, don't
do no good, them no help f'children hospitals,
Deciduous Hills-n-Shortshift, Coniferous Reaches—
. . . only place left Evelyn hasn't fallen in yet,
is th'last try children's hospital, Abuse . . . strike
horror inna young child's heart, they cut your
hair off there, make you go every place in diapers

so Evelyn been bein' good, takin' maybe only one hit
when her knees banjo if she don't . . . she gettin' it,
Buffer suspect, from one a th' high school custodians,
who couldn't get laid f'himself . . . Buffer find him
he be walkin' on his elbows . . . but th'real thing makin'
Buffer-n-Charlene Rose mad, th'new school of Psychologist
says to Buffer-n-Charlene, Evelyn not a victim of
Statutory Rape even if Pinhead th'sailor who fucked her
four or five times, a 30-year-old man did come before
custodian-n-he diddled her tit nipples hard 'til
they send shortwave messages, a 30-year-old grown man

arouse sensual ache to be fulfilled in
her so she come back agin-n-agin f'more of
this jest wunnerful thing! . . . yet Buffer
tell me he sit in Coniferous Reaches hospital
where children go, listenin' to a male
Psychologist look him right inna eye-n-tell
him that he knows th'law don' agree with him but

he does not feel what Buffer's daughter Evelyn
participate in is "rape," he consider it rape
only if girl is forced . . . in other words
Evelyn age 13, seduce th'grown man . . . men.

Wimmen responsible f'all sex! . . . in other
words th'fuckin' of a naturally curious
adolescent 13-, 14-year old child not by another
13-, 14-year-old child but by a grown man
is not to this Psychologist Statutory Rape
-n-I'm about t'really go drinkin' agin when
I'm hearin' another thing wrong with America,
not clearheaded enough to think, it isn't
jest in America sumthin' like this'd be wrong,
-n-that isn't what should be concernin' me but
what attitude has come to in my country.

-n-I'm about t'go really drinkin' when I'm hearin'
this from m'old buddy Buffer . . . I
went drinkin' . . . Nobody's fault . . . A
drinker can't blame anyone. Cure lies in us
I jest couldn't stop. I didn't want to . . .
You must want to. I'm inna situation lissenin'
t'Buffer Rose who come over got me at my house
before Mrs. Bop got home from her steady-payin'
good job as a Parole Officer . . . Buffer get me to
a six-pack of ice-cold ale in his car, sippin'
while he's tellin' me about Evelyn, he, Buffer th'biggest

fucker you ever saw of anythin' with a hole
cryin' his insides out when it's his Evelyn
we talkin' 'bout got fucked . . . prob'ly got taught to
suck it too, though neither Buffer or I say that
right out, 'though once that all me-n-Buffer
like, though 'course y'd never marry a girl who

would-n-til that Deep Throat come out inna movies
y'wondered how y'd ever bring sumthin' like that up
t'Mrs.-n-never dared to . . . Y'd hint, but one look
from Mrs. Bop-n-I never suggest it agin-n-I don't think
Buffer did either . . . Y'd say to Mrs. . . . we oughta go

check out what's Deep Throat . . . but one look from Mrs.
. . . we had to make it on our memories . . . Now here-m-I
sippin' agin with m'memory, at this same time I'm
th'Father of 15-year-old Lollibop-here-m-I Bop rememberin'
girls I took inna car's back seat,took 'em out for no
other reason, me 14, with my ass beat so hard at home
by Housekeeper I had to fuck for my
very survival cock weapon and savage into girls.
Th'girls loved it, I keep tellin' m'self now . . .
Loved it, waited for us to come in our car every
Thursday night when we'd drive-n-do it-n-go

dancin'-n-do it again 'fore we took 'em home
but way deep in me was a dirty feelin'-n-I'd
laugh nervous like it would go away if you
jest went ha ha ha ha w'd drown out, throttle
th'awful feelin' you were a coward only offerin'
a girl a good time if she'd put out . . . It was
a frightenin' feelin' of self-disgust . . . yet
lust come back-n-you'd do it agin-n-agin-agin . . .
Laughin' thinkin' of Roberta-n-how I
had her turned around on her hands
-n-knees and took her whisperin', plunged

in whisperin' inner ear thisis how everybody do it . . .
. . . cold sweat, Bop memory . . . victim vengeance memory
now not wantin' it t'ever happen t'Lollibop knowin'
y'gut it cummin'f'whut y'done.
Bop drinkin' . . . Everythin' overwhelmin' . . . America

I loved-n-unnerstood . . . where!?, where is it!?
Mother, we'll meet again. I will tell you I love you then.
. . . for carrying little constantly shitting me
around in your arms all the time as long
as you could. Crude as I turned out, whatever
softness, grace, compassion, courage I have is

from your cuddling me and talking to me, telling me
you loved me although I don't remember it. I know it.
I know you did . . . Mother, when we meet I will tell you
I love you for my first years walked by you, talked to
by you, instilled with the only love I ever knew but
it was enough to clip the mass murderer in me . . . Mother. . .
. . . I went drinkin' agin, me, Bop . . .
Screams somewhere in the boozing.
Drink with anyone . . . Hobozo mass
murderer, old friend, doesn't matter.
The neon's on. The bottles are splashing

your soul into the dark corners of calm
doom . . . He's got a quart, I've got a
dollar. We put the town under beer suds . . .
Wandering on the slippery peeling
to bars to someone's house. Sitting
hunched over wet brown bags in
freezing somebody's car vulnerable
to be knifed or suffocated and vanished
for the ale-stained cash loose in shirt
pocket or crumpled around keys. Worse
horror is you live and do not die when

you are numb blotted on the world your
sweat tossing the water of you onto cold
day, but dry out frightened and down.

Weak and frail lost to everything. All the
faces of your drinking partners blurred in
your retching. There are no good friends of the glass.
. . . Is that it!? . . . You're not makin' it, Bop,
even here in Little Hope any more than
you made it outside in society, no you didn't!
Couldn't function again and again . . . can't
blame Lollibop, can't blame anyone . . .

    . . . Bop heard Lucy Bubblegum say, it
    seemed from far away . . . "I think he's
    handling himself well." The real
    nurses exchanged looks . . . Right there
    with wife and Lucy Bubblegum, Bop got the
    feeling nurses weren't "certain"
    same treatment's for everyone . . . Bop
    . . . bewildered staggering drunk found
    himself part of a "Community" of people
    he'd shake like fleas outside. By the time
    you leave Little Hope your face has its stamp.

III

. . . Hands reaching in through ground floor
bedroom windows and stabbing our
children to death . . . You're lying
asleep in your bed, a hand reaches in
and plunges death into your chest.
What about the unstable parents
of the child, how do you live through
your own child's call to you for help? . . . and
you came rushing . . . but the blade of the
knife had already killed her. How do
parents survive waking up out of

———

sound sleep to screams of their progeny
already killed but calling to you and
asking Daddy, not for Frowning Boo-Boo
the Teddy Bear, but for her life? She
knows she is dead. She's too young
to realize it. And you see the blood
spurting goodbye to you. Your own
child's blood is running away.
The red blood of your infant
is running out. Just an hour ago
she had almost a Century. Now she

does not have a minute. But you have
and how will you live the minutes
wondering over and over how you
could not have failed your child
who called out to you in her last breath?
You'll go over in your mind every evil
you ever did and convince yourself you
had this coming, just so you can live
with it . . . or you will never live with it.
You'll hit everything that moves and really drink.
Killing yourself desperately in despair.

The mother will never get over it.
No one will matter now, her baby is dead.
Yes, they'll "get" Hobozo, "he" will slip,
he undoubtedly wants to get caught, he's a
Harvard man who one day will become tired of
what he's become or get carefully careless . . .
The sneering, chortling snicker chuckling
will whimper in him; he is sick. The poor
ender of my daughter's whole life is ill and

it will be learned that it *was known* that "this"
Hobozo was very murderously dangerously available,

free . . . the tragedy will come out that he
wasn't meant to be loose on us, to get the
chance to reach in his arm through the
bedroom window of young girls with a knife
in his hand . . . and it will be learned that
in the millions of details and paperwork that
it seems to take to handle sick people, this Hobozo
was known, let out of hospital because
no one could snap a phone call about him
to anyone responsible . . . don't let this
Hobozo out, he's a killer . . . and so

young girls didn't even have a chance.
He'll reach his arm in through the
bedroom window of our young children
and stab them to death . . . yet must be
forgiven because we knew him, somebody
did . . . but it all got lost in paperwork . . .
Why does he do this . . . is there this way
to make love that orgasms by the sudden
surprise death of my child in her bed for
Hobozos stalking our nights as if their
penises are invisibly wired to knife blades? . . .

. . . Murderer stalking children to snuff
them out from pain he knows or to kill them
little before they grow hairbrush hands . . . This
Hobozo beside Boppledock in the rowboat of suds,
bought barroom companion. A flash from killing
Bop too but cunningly realizing the cover right
in front of everyone's eyes sitting and talking

and drinking free on this fat fool's coin . . . bright
Harvard graduate in self-destruction . . . He
can't stand to succeed, he's brilliant,
understands the schemes, whores

other people are, whore he is
become sarcastic in his illness,
into Soup Kitchens when he
isn't locked up to prevent
himself from himself . . . or . . . children . . .
while he bums you he senses you sense
something about him, it's in his eyes
that do not think you "see" them . . . it's
in his illness to think only he "sees"
and he is missed by everyone, by police
searching for the killer, even the

doctors who know him best and are reading
the slaughter over quick breakfast of a
fast coffee and a roll before making
rounds of the ward he should be on . . . miss
him . . . it's too true to be true . . . he is
missed until his death is done, he still
breathing blended into Soup Kitchen
naturally hidden from last murder because
none of them make sense and he's killed
and is back mopping for Father The Priest or
he cuts himself again just enough to

get committed and so psychiatrically
diagnosed as destructive to himself not
others, safe inside while the heavy
manhunt looks ruthlessly for him but
cannot find him and then he does not kill
immediately, there is a warmth, pleasure

in his Harvard brightness reading *The
New York Times* and even the *Daily News*
theory as one of half-a-hundred
in a chair in the Soup Kitchen silent or
cleverly better, mutters to himself.

having him a conversation that everyone
including Police walk right by dismissing
him as the knifer. He's no one's
preconceived idea and so gets away.
He bums you as much to irritate as for
any need . . . cigarettes . . . alcohol, when
he can slink to it out of your sight
in cunning of realize you visualize him
downing wine not stabbing . . . he hides
behind laughter bitter at itself he uses
to protect himself from what Cambridge,

Massachusetts required him to realize as
our probable opinion of people with no
commitment. He drops famous names as
family friends and they well may be
friends of his family but they're
not his friends and his bitterness
is almost crying, heaving his
hurt heart into somewhat of a
foolish giggle telling you he
phoned them and they told him
to go get a job . . . that's very

funny to him, reassuring himself
in these calls, in perhaps a note
to someone home sometimes that
there's nothing for him there
if he wanted to stop the killing,

no one at home says come home. No
one wants him where he came from . . .
He laughs in your face, amused
you don't know how many children
will never grow up, excited by
what he thinks you might do in

your tearing him limb from limb it's
almost wonderful!!, the thought to him.
He is an intelligent man and no one
knows better than he what he has become.
There are moments when he is horrified,
recalls boyhood, the rage which he
had to find to survive. Survive?
Why kill strangers then, why not
the people who killed his life before
it began . . . it's all twisted in him
because . . . he loves children!

In Saint Vincent de Paul Place Soup Kitchen,
men and women look as if the day stuck to them.
Smell the rhubarb of them surviving as scavenger
or into Soup Kitchen for food, companionship.
Hobozo stalks rubbish, robber of our skeletons.
Hovering in dilapidated abandoned neighborhood
where the wino in rags fears for his life. The
dust that is left on the earth of the dead blows
away until the yesterdays of Post Cards are gone.
All the towns are run from and we are in fright
of charity. Downtown moved out of town.

IV

. . . You are someone who has not functioned
in society . . . the game here is to get you

as you come in, while you are just arrived,
confused, flipped, to "write a contract" . . . a
confession against yourself, to sign forms
so they can tell you you "agreed to" abuse,
to be ridiculed, to be judged by other Illys . . .
but they don't surround you with
liquor or Heroin the way you will
be surrounded the instant you leave
Little Hope . . . no, "theory" is you

haven't functioned in society
again and again, time after time,
so, make your life miserable with
criticism, humiliation, ridicule, which
signed forms read you say you agree to,
but the thing is you really didn't, wouldn't
have in good shape, so they're setting you
up as much as you're already set to find
drink as soon as you can again . . . Cure lies
in us. They get you to write a confession
against yourself, sincerity of which is

estimated at how much of a deceiver you
reveal you are and *maybe you* are, but the
human next to you may have really tried out
there in real world, really struggled, worked,
supported people . . . Suddenly his job world
collapsed, vanished and he is entering
middle age a weakling, admittedly, unable
to control urges, urge to shoot, urge to
drink . . . and he or she may be young in a
world with no base, no clear direction . . . Now
Bop is honest enough to write out for

them what they would not know of him to

use against his already disturbed inner
state if he did not come out and tell
them those things of battered childhood
and heartbreak he somehow survived
through day when Father would scream
"There's nuthin' Gawdam wrong with you
but y'lazy arse which I whipped with a
switch from a good birch tree I let you
pick out yourself as Gawd directed me to—
doin' m'duty by you but look whut you become!

"*Look* at you! You ain't no son a'mine! If you
do this you are on your own!" Here in Little
Hope Hospital where you'd hoped for Individual
help from somebody possibly qualified, the
idea is to irritate you so you'll "act" . . . so
you'll never want to ever come back to *this*
place! But you hardly will if you're cured . . . if
you can control your urge . . . "Making you over"
teaching you to tell on everyone, to "bring up"
in group half-overheard personal telephone
conversations, which the one you listened

in on is expected to relish "revealing" to
everyone . . . it puts a stamp on faces, creates
illness where none existed, where a Heroin
habit existed . . . where an alcohol habit existed
but where telling on someone, and yourself
was always reprehensible, now you're supposed
to because . . . because you "haven't been
interinvolving with society" . . . haven't been
able to respond, haven't been being responsible,
so "theory" here is that a Community of ill
people can judge each other, one is to be made

over, haven't been able to stay sober, cease
suicide attempt, stop th'snortin' . . . as you are . . .
now one is to become a snitch on oneself and
anyone else in "The Community" a half-overheard
telephone conversation you're having, you "thought"
privately, brought up in Community Meeting, that
from what was "overheard" by Community member Toothpick
In Featherhat The Farter, evidently you don't like
it here . . . community ill person, ill as you are and
now, here, medication crushing snorting Toothpick In
Featherhat The Farter allowed to bring up what might

be so private from your outside real world as to
do you serious damage by being made to discuss it
with people who haven't been able to function in
real world time after time, again and again . . . Bludgeon,
Motorcycle gang sodomist here awaiting upcoming trial so
good lawyer can advise court that this here Bludgeon has
changed, joined "Community Group"
hoping that Little Hope will get him
back out on th'street to "scan th'man, man! to
rob and drink and snort an' git kyik!"
sodomizing, killin', hittin', stompin', that

th'life, ye-ah! . . . in hyre, in hyre, Little
Hope a joke! Lotsa deadbeat lotsa fucks oughta
be wasted save sassiety feedin' 'em man! Now
me Blud-geon! I look inna mirror an' say
I be right back! Ye-ah! I do I do I do . . .
Bludgeon is now "makin' hissef over" Yippie!!
lak his lawyer say, man! Interactin' they
callsit when otheren peeple (he might
usually mayhem) . . . outside . . . outside a'hyre
Bludgeon in business with Toothpick In Featherhat
Th'Farter . . . Th' Fierce-White Bike Collectors whoo-whee!-n-

——

Toothpick In Featherhat Th'Farter's wommen Arlene
-n-Bludgeon's deary Dixie find th'word Alzheimer's
disease inna newspaper and th'other afternoon afore
Bludgeon picked up-n-his lawyer say "better be
Little Hope," this old lady she's walkin' downa street
toward her son's house an' by th'time she got to th'corner
she couldn't remember anythin' an' jes then's when
Arlene join her, poor old thing, she gets lost on buses,
lost—Arlene walk along beside her-n-within a block
ole Lady Lotte think she have a new frien' . . .
. . . Soon deary Dixie pull up by them inna car,

in minutes all three inna car. They ride aroun'.
Then Arlene tell ole Lotte she need to cash a
check f'Four Thousan' dollars . . . It from
someplace call National Auto Service, Seattle,
Washington . . . could dear ole Lotte hep them ut?
Do she have a bank nearby? Do she have money inna
bank? Yes there is an account at The Trusting Trust,
nex' stop th'bank. While Arlene-n-deary Dixie wait
inna car, dear ole Alzheimer Lotte go in her bank. A
few minutes later she come out witha deposit slip.
No no no no no, Arlene explain, there a mistake—

check not t'be deposit-t-be cashed! This time a
Teller explain t'poor bewildered dear ole Lotte
th'check cannot be cash until it clear . . . only
way to do it now would be to cash in against her life
savings account-n-she, poor dear ole Lotte's only got
Four Thousand Two Hundred dollars in her life savings
account . . . Uhhuh! Thet's how she do play! Yippie!!-n-
Bludgeon-n-Toothpick In Featherhat Th'Farter ridin'
roun' on motorcycles in full cycle rigs, roar aroun'

town tryin' t'collect money owed f'rent, bad check,
court judgment . . . Th'Throttle City Credit Collection

Bureau admire Bludgeon-n-Toothpick In
Featherhat Th'Farter . . . its records show 3.5 million
in bad checks durin' Reagan paradise-n-Bludgeon-n-
Toothpick In Featherhat Th'Farter a credit to credit
collection . . . Ridin' roun', Bludgeon he wear a
turquoise ringin his ear, a bandanna roun' his shoulder
length hair, a tattoo of a wommen's nice bare bottom
in th'flex of his arm muscle . . . Toothpick In Featherhat
Th'Farter he wear a bandanna too tied roun' his
head, leather vest unner his jacket . . . He-n-
Bludgeon look f'all th'world like they might

break your arm, but Toothpick In Featherhat
Th'Farter, he say, in High School English, they
jes' "look tough," their appearance hep th'Fierce-White
Bike Company business by encouragin' peeple
t'pay up th'money they owe . . . It Bludgeon's
idea . . . When he bounce a few checks hissef
while recoverin' from a tummy fulla knife
an' couldn't get about much, collection
agencies didn't try very hard to collect he
discover . . . but Bludgeon lak his butt fuckin'
no matter how much deary Dixie give him her

nice fat bare bottom 'cause he make her-n-thet
gettim inta trouble, gettim arrested-n-facin'
serious prison . . . Bludgeon lak a good man onceinnawhile-n-
all'ays hav' Toothpick In Featherhat Th'Farter
but Toothpick In Featherhat Th'Farter don' never
givim too much onna outside, 'less Bludgeon he
start singin' Th'Star Spangled Banner-n-talkin'

t'im 'bout th'Flag, allegiance, *then* Toothpick
In Featherhat Th'Farter all'ays givim his ass,
Toothpick a loyal patriot, all'ays go f'follow
th'leader-n-Bludgeon his leader but Bludgeon he

don' do thet much, he don' believe in nuthin' 'sides
Bludgeon he don' really never wanner put his lovely
tallywhacker in where them farts of Toothpick In
Featherhat th'Farter cum from, but Bludgeon'll
do it willin' rather than completely go without
yesindeedie . . . n-Toothpick In Featherhat Th'Farter
is th'perfect trick, sidekick . . . in hyre, now when they
in Little Hope, Toothpick In Featherhat Th'Farter
shrewd, play act like he nut in court, in fact,
Toothpick In Featherhat Th'Farter's kinda surprised
he don' feel he have t'act or do much different-n-he

all'ays is—only thing not to ever make Bludgeon mad while
they in Little Hope any more-n-deary Dixie do when
they onna outside-n-if-n-when deary Dixie out
Alzheimerin' bes' thing t'do is always let
Bludgeon do whut Bludgeon he wanna . . . th'heat
come-n-git Bludgeon who true to his loyalty
immediately involve Toothpick In Featherhat Th'
Farter, for he, Bludgeon, ain' goin' nowhere
without his screwin' business associate (it all right
deary Dixie know 'bout him-n-Toothpick In Featherhat Th'
Farter-n-thet they do whatever Bludgeon wanna-n-she

relieved! 'leas' it ainna 'nother wommen!)—Now Bludgeon
cool, now he, Bludgeon brings up in Little Hope "Group"
that he knows, Bop, your phone conversation is private but
Toothpick, hyre, en Featherhat Th'Farter . . . (who gonna
be anice piecea ass inner sheets tonight after lights out
when you can tiptoe th'corridor past them desk sucks

or jes' wouldn't be *no* good at breakin'-n-enterin' . . . he,
Blud-geon good at "enterin' " alright . . . all'ays easy with
this cocaine-snortin' squealer chicken sucker, th'blade
of a small penknife right on Featherhat Th'Farter's vein in
in his neck while he worked his legs up onto his shoulders

and plunged in "smop" in, chug, chug, not a sound outa Featherhat,
he know who fuckin' him . . . what go down in Little Hope-n-what
don't) . . . Now it time to mess up a few weirdo lose 'em
some "steps" except that fat gray man, that Bop, he alright!
He "regular" come roun' talk "decent" t'Blud-geon lak he know
who Bludgeon! Still gotta back Toothpick en Featherhat th'Farter . . .
. . . Now y'phone conversation . . . Farter say he hear you tellin'
somebody how this place f'nuts-n-junkie . . . and without blinking
you better be able to churp to "Group" something! You know, Bop
. . . make it up . . . This is just some more
hustle . . . what you have to do in real

world too . . . lay it brother! . . . like
how the person on the other end of the phone
was maybe Long Time Charlie who did 7
years' hard time for driving someplace
drunk and runnin' over somebody who didn't
die and liquor caused his action because
he wouldn't have done it otherwise, just
being 3 days out right now from 5 he
done for slippin' in a liquor store with
a thirty-eight goin' off just as
twirling red bulbs drive by . . . and he's

been begging you pleeze, Boppledock, by all
th' saints that luvya and all *that* "Staff"
almost vomits hearing . . . pleeze, Bop, turn
yourself into a wonderfully psychiatrically
oriented hospital and that's what you

were telling him you had! Now "Group"
beams at you. George, a middle-ager with
boozer forever etched in his look, looks
at you and it's three oranges time! "I
haven't liked you, Bop, from the first
second you came in here, now I do."

. . . There's dead silence. This is
Little Hope working! See! See! See what
"Staff's" been trying to tell you happens
when, when you tell the truth and come out
with pure interrelating!! . . . It's *wonderful*!!!
George didn't like you, now he likes you!!!
and it was all because Toothpick In Featherhat
The Farter took a chance at offending you,
intruded on your privacy? . . . maybe! maybe! but
you *shared* and now look at Farty! (His sneak
eyes don't know what they see, so Staff

tells him) and Bop gets up, looks sheepish,
crosses and shakes George's hand and Blu-dgeon
looks at Bop with admiration . . . "Boy do dat dude
lay down a good rap!" . . . Bludgeon naturally loves
anyone who gets out of things, especially if
he's been "set up" like he and Toothpick In
Featherhat The Farter just tried to cost
Bop "steps" if they could . . . now
AA Counselor nodding approval, looking
around at everyone, see, see what's
happening right here now this instant!?

"See the reason for 'Group,' see how we
share and tell and get well!? Boppledock's
shared with us even what everyone in the
room knows was a *private* telephone

conversation, but," her head looks like it's
turning a circle on her neck, "nothing's
private here, got to give all that over to
Little Hope Hospital" . . . We know what's best!
Your face everyone will "see" when you
leave us may have a look on it of having
witnessed some head-on collision, your

natural instinctive makeup so worked on by
us that the "look" in your face is sickness to
anyone outside in outside real world who
does not know what you were like when you
came in to Little Hope after being unable to
function in society again and again, time
after time . . . You will look cracked, even
barely able to hold yourself together
to *them*—to *them*! But they aren't *you*,
weren't you, were they!!? You are better able
to try not to ever do those things

again that brought you here, aren't you!?
. . . our "theory" here is that a "Community"
of ill people can "spot the con" everyone's
always lived by, in each other, one is to
become a snitch on oneself and anyone
else . . . tell tell tell! Accusation is
enough to get reevaluated by your
ill patient "community" and "Staff," no one
even "has to *see* something," like your
climbing out the window of your room
to smoke or go to nearby liquor store . . .

So old Bop has a week he's paying for
wasted of what was supposed to be therapy
helping *him*, while Bludgeon and Toothpick

In Featherhat The Farter twist "Group's"
honor theory system of "confessing," fellows
who have hurt people for heroin . . . When
Bludgeon and Toothpick In Featherhat The
Farter went out a window, who knows, to
suck a roach under a tree in wild bronc
moonlight, drink, who knows, and got back
inside Little Hope without being "seen"

no one "actually saw" them, Toothpick In
Featherhat The Farter had to go "tell"
Suicidal Lucille . . . here, too, at
Little Hope are those who "say" they
attempted suicide . . . If you yourself
were "well" you'd "see" that here
at Little Hope none of the light bulbs
are covered up or closets of cleaner
padlocked, many ways anyone could cut
out their life or swallow it, this
isn't any deep lockup . . . Little Hope

irked Suicidal Lucille who looked at you with
agate eyes with strange lure in them,
like being excited by the dead or
sniffing scent long gone, like
"nobody'll ever have *me*," serenely smiling
telling in Group how the first try
was the hardest, every other gets
easier and easier . . . Suicidal Lucille
felt "honor bound" to "tell Group" that
Bludgeon and Farty had slipped out of
Little Hope for a taste . . . Instantly

Mr. Adrenalin, Doc Prune's Business
Manager, whispered like a deaf undertaker

that Community Group is not a democracy,
not a place of innocence, innocent until
proven guilty . . . the brave patient who would
march against KKK better stick to his
Librium here . . . Now here's Bop in a situation
where nobody "saw" anyone go out a window . . .
. . . only Suicidal Lucille who hates Bludgeon
and Farty for what their kind have done in
her briefs . . . no one "saw" anyone go out a window

and climb back in or drink or suck or snort and
"Staff" says if whoever did it "had any guts"
they'd come right out and tell on themselves
and right here is the big flaw in Little
Hope "theory" . . . because "telling" will
not result in "hoo-ray reward" the gift of a
"step," "congratulations" for having slipped
but owning up . . . no, telling will result in
"reevaluation" to "zero" from "step" "14"!?
Only the *very* ill will do *that* to themselves . . .
. . . not Bludgeon or Toothpick In Featherhat The Farter.

V

Poor dear lovely tiny Irish lady
trying to figure out why her
husband went to work the day she
almost killed herself, that to him
it was like any other day he had to
go out and support them, until she
looked so bad to him he brought her
to Little Hope hoping . . . one who can
still cry, still break into tears,
perhaps can be turned from what is
true, she *is* suicidal . . . the small

———

Irish lady, such a beautiful lost
tiny thing who talks hesitatingly
. . . "I told him I was suicidal before
we got married! I told him and yet
he went to work that day just the same!
We had our extension phone put in our
bedroom" (she's painting the air with
her fingers) . . . "That was my life line" . . .
(reflectively gazing into herself . . .
no one else but her was here in the
room now, no one else sick here) . . . "He

still went to work that day."—"My name's
Bop," I spoke up and asked . . . "You mean to
tell us that because you told him you
might kill yourself before he married
you, that means he's supposed to
always be around waiting for it or
to stop you, how could he do that
and stay sane!?" . . . "No, no" she
cries and real tears come, then
tossing her head defiantly . . . "I've
told him not to come to visit here,

not to call me on the telephone or
come until I've worked it out just
what I think of him" . . . I said
(You're supposed to give feedback in
"Group" or you can't get your "steps"
in Community vote) . . . "What you've
just said sounds like a child who's
angry at a spanking and being sent
to bed without supper because she

told her mother she's liable to
steal cookies after school, just before

supper" . . . "No, No!" she sobs, jumps up
and dashes out of the room and because
"Staff" knows you aren't going to
endure this "patient-curing-patient"
theory, the specific personal attack,
insult, criticism called "making you
over" to make you "see" you as you never
"saw" you before, but are going to
sign yourself out against medical
advice from Little Hope; because old
Boppledock, son of Mom and Dad who

flapped their way through th'20s
is going back into the fight real life is,
now "Staff"—though always up to now they've
marked down whether you've "participated"
in "Group" or not, given positive or
negative "feedback": now the half-trained
observer who oversees "Group" savagely
attacks you, because you're leaving and if
he can make you break down you'd "see" for
yourself you're in no condition to go back
to real life . . . and then he can give you

love, even his admiration, even commend you
in "Group" and to Charge Nurse and to "Staff"
but not *now*! Not *now*! Not with you doing
what you're going to do, go back to real
life realizing that cure lies in ourselves . . .
or in us with Psychiatrist and you getting at
your disturbance, not here in the open tomb

Little Hope Hospital . . . When the little Irish
lady, so tiny, so pretty, comes back
into the room from "you just don't
understand us suicides" and you

apologize publicly to help group of
Illys hear you say you're sorry, you
didn't mean to drive her to leave the
room, were only responding to her as
everyone there has felt quite free to
lay on you whatever vicious remarks
occur to them, and some were very good,
true, helpful because you wish to see
yourself get well . . . and because you
meant the poor woman no harm . . . but
half-trained observer really jumps you.

A week ago he would have pursed his
lips pained expression told you you
should do a lot of listening, after
all, you haven't been able to function
in society again and again, time after
time . . . you should do a lot more listening
than talking . . . Then a week ago he
would have soothed . . . "but you
made some good points!! good good
for involving!" and he would have asked
weeping suicidal . . . "What do you think

of Boppledock's statement? Are you
angry because your husband wasn't
right there just the day you
might have killed yourself?" She's
not even listening . . . She doesn't
comprehend anyone in the room . . . not

Toothpick In Featherhat The Farter, not
Bludgeon, not Boppledock, not Suicidal
Lucille . . . She doesn't "realize" that
half-trained observer has savagely
gone after Bop because he's not

going to endure this anymore . . . "Su-suppose
I just didn't bother to pick up the
telephone that noon . . . when he called me.
We were laughing and I giggled . . . but
suppose I just didn't answer the phone . . ."
She's furious because she is now allowing
herself to feel that he went to work
either not really caring for her, loving
her or worse, not believing she'd do it
and she's in here in Little Hope Hospital
because she got herself worked into a

state that he saw she might do it and so did
the best he could think to do then,
brought her to Little Hope . . . So what
happens to you, dear Bop, even
to Toothpick In Featherhat The
Farter . . . to toothpick-chewing
cocaine-medication-snorting Farty-
Featherhat . . . is you're here
for help, beginning to crack so
everyone's "noticing"—to find
yourself not getting "individual"

attention to what your specific
illness may be . . . First you're
in "Detox" in alcoholic's irrational
self-pity, unable to "realize" clearly,
then soon as your blood pressure and

heart lower and slow, in a "program"
of patients set upon each other,
"Community" of Illys who could
vote against what you really need
easily, since they, too, are sick, haven't
been able to function in society

again and again, time after time, so
injure you, you injured by this "patient-
curing-patient" theory therapy, you
become worse than when—when you got
to Little Hope's group of many kinds
of ill people called "A Community"
of Manic Depressives, Suicidals,
Addicts, even Motorcycle gang
mentalities here now to help
themselves in court whether
Bludgeon and Toothpick In

Featherhat The Farter do or do not tell
on themselves, the accusation against
them is believed by "Staff," by Mr.
Adrenalin, by Lucy Bubblegum . . . Bop
saw the street gang run the place
while Social Worker stuttered . . .
Lucy Bubblegum glared . . . and those who
had rammed Little Hope Hospital down
Bop sat perplexed . . . it happened
in the middle of the night, like a Billy-Jo
romance . . . "Daddy don' blow his arse away

we gonner shoot her-oin" kind of thing . . .
Toothpick In Featherhat The Farter's girl
Arlene told him no more! Goo-bye!
Bludgeon c'd have him, that dunnit!

T'hell with Little Hope, Toothpick In
Featherhat The Farter now his ole sef,
he had to git out unner a prairie dog
sky agin now, not later, now and
Bludgeon betteren not thinkin' he goin'
t'be on top all th'time no more, no sir!
Thinking this, deciding this excited

Toothpick In Featherhat The Farter and
Blud-geon like aggression, *sometimes* . . . how
you goin' t'feel gooud-n-enjoy whut y'do
t'someone you know, make 'em do 'less you
know whut it feel like an' so no one in
Th'Thrillers motorcycle gang or th'Fierce-White
Bike Company c'd ever say, Bludgeon he "do it"
but couldn't "take it!" . . . only thang y'cain't "take"
is bein' murdered ahaha! Yippie! Bludgeon he
snuck to liquor store and now in "Group"
Lucy Bubblegum looking at Bop and beautiful

tiny Irish lady with vomit in her bland head,
is excited by Bludgeon and Toothpick In
Featherhat The Farter . . . They're at least
"honest," HONEST!!? . . . well at least they're
who they are! Lucy Bubblegum senses a vague
groin ache like lust is the spoils of violence . . .
. . . "Do it to me . . .!" . . . always the music in our
secret thoughts . . . She is drawn by a cruel
line in Bludgeon's lip and his eyes
darting, finding Lucy Bubblegum
breathing hot in Little Hope . . .

VI

Father, Bop is wandering! Washington

Irving, you struck our vein, we are
narcoleptic and love fantasy . . . ghost
stories and cheap romance while we
pull covers up over our heads, the
dead calling to us the American
dream is ending . . . now our government
thinks the worst of people . . . no
longer in America, my Father, is there
belief people will do well out of love . . .
. . . we must go find our original wish

in the Cosmos and in ourselves . . . Stephen
Crane, by creating yourself in "The Blue
Hotel" as the character called "The
Easterner," "Mr. Blanc," like blank, no
mark on this guy, the Easterner, the
Easterner a person who is empty, untouched . . .
. . . Could "The Easterner" (Stephen Crane) be
telling us that all his brief twenty-eight-year
life he is not a participator . . . never served
in The Civil War or wandered New York
City's Bowery . . . things he wrote about . . . but

finally near his end, finally participated,
involved, invested himself, his soul in his dream? . . .
. . . Blanc means white, then . . . whitewash?—Peeping
Tom standing back from . . . is what Americans are . . .?
Stephen Crane come to John Donne realization when,
finally as his character The Easterner confronts the
Cowboy in "The Blue Hotel" and tells him that they each
and every one of them, all of them were responsible for
the death of The Swede . . . What of America is guilty of Bop
death if Bop was not a struggler, now, Boppledock, your son,
Father, wanders through living in swallows of blackout.

———

Mother, you died on me and left me.
I always thought you'd be back . . . when I
was Eight I did. When I was Nine I did. You
were just away with another boy who needed
you more than I did . . . Mother, we are each
other! You and I are each other! . . . and I
have never forgotten you, even though your
face is just a vague flash smiling up
at me when I was only seven and Big Billy
brought Young Billy and me to see you in
your hospital bed because in your dying

delirium you'd asked him to let you see us
once more. I really didn't understand that
this was the last time I was ever going to
see you and when Big Billy came to the
bottom of the backstairs below our bed-
room and called up to us that you wouldn't
be coming home (he couldn't come up to
tell us, to hold us and tell us, he had to
call the news up to us) . . . Somehow Young
Billy seemed to comprehend it, age only
six, he burst into tears, but I was too

dumb and too numb to comprehend and you
died two days before Christmas so no one
knew what to tell me with Christmas and
Santa Claus joy just about to come, so,
someone looked at Big Billy, an aunt, a
sister of yours, and I wasn't wondering
why everyone was there, Big Billy sisters
and your sister, even if it was Christmas,
never that I can remember had so many
of my aunts and uncles and their children,
our cousins, everyone been there at

———

Christmas before, of course I was only
Seven and dreamed a lot, got lost in my
thoughts—even then, but I wasn't wondering!
. . . *why* so many people were there . . .
and suddenly Big Billy put us with a
family who lived across the street, it
was all so puzzling, wasn't it Christmas
and weren't we going to have Christmas in
our own home . . .? I watched my chance and
I escaped, I got by whoever in the neigh-
bor family was supposed to be keeping an

eye on me and Young Billy and I ran to
my house, the house Young Billy and me
were supposed to be in and I got by an
empty kitchen into a dining room to half-
closed parlor doors and I slipped in and
there was an odor of purple violets like
in no air and there you were lying down
with your hands folded on your chest,
like you were asleep, so it was always
easy for me to believe that you'd gone
away to take care of a little boy who

needed you more than I did because I knew
I have to lie down and go to sleep! I had
seen you asleep! Suddenly bursting people
all around me and I knew I'd done something
wrong, but no one touched me, everyone
seemed to want to see what I was going to
do, well, once I'd seen you, Mother, I went
back to the neighbor's family blissfully
and I always gave it to Big Billy, he made

a Christmas for us then, no matter what
was going on in his heart.

Mother, you and I have never parted. We
are always each other . . . but men and
women are at strategy with each other
devising ways to manipulate . . . maleness,
femaleness—strategies of reproduction
differing in psychology and structure,
each pursuing differently the achievement
of life . . . The danger to love is if the
act is considered a favor women perform
for men . . . even when women are believed
to get more pleasure . . . We are strangers,

Mother, in our very sex, for while I work
seriously and hard to undo the male chauvin-
ism inbred in me as my male right, all the
while, still, the truth is that the best way
to maximize your genes' representation in
the next generation was to lay Big Billy!
Look! I am *you*, Mother. I want to be you.
We are each other. Yes, I'm many people and
I talk, sometimes slang, like when I'm with
Buffer Rose inna bar-n-we're discussin' . . .
I've many voices and I'm many people and so

is everyone, if they'd only realize it, Mother!
I've been promiscuous. I've done some filthy
things. I'm a human being! I'm not sorry
any more than you are for picking Father,
exactly! for "being choosy" who you let
give you the seed of me. I want to be you,
Mother, I want to live the life robbed from

you young for you . . . I was worth bearing to
you, Mother, because you knew I carry half
your genes . . . The price men pay for being
spared pregnancy is the possibility the

child isn't his, no—I do not believe Big
Billy did not think I am his son, it's the
way you two did it and then had to get
married because I was in you, Mother, and
Big Billy had no choices under those day
codes and while forever and always exclaiming
"What a swell girl" you were, he never forgave
me, Mother—I changed his secret desire's
course—he had planned to fuck and run!—I've
done it myself, Mother, but in a different
time . . . Mother, Father "didn't realize his

mind." "Minds that want what the male wants
are the kind we're likely to find if we look"
—as Edwin Osborne Wilson notes—"because
that's the kind of mind whose genes get
multiplied the most"—And Osborne reminds
"We should realize that a mind like ours,
which evolves by selection is constructed
to promote the survival of the genes that
created it,—not to understand itself!"—When
I was Fourteen alone in my room, my bedroom,
your room, it had been your room when you were

a girl in that house and it was my room, I used
to almost think that I smelled you in it. Once
I swear you appeared to me there in the black
dark and told me, whispered to me to always be a
good boy . . . and I knew I would be deep in me if
I hadn't had all those beatings from nineteen-

year-old Housekeeper that broke me like
thread, everything become so overwhelming
for me forever, but I swear, Mother, that
you came to me in that room that was my
bedroom that had been your room, when I was

fourteen and you asked me to be a good boy
and I knew I hadn't been being very good, out
into every girl I could, because I was
big now and nineteen-year-old Housekeeper
was being careful but I was getting even
with any and every girl I could get back at
and then coming back into my room and
"making believe" I was with you and you were
with me . . . Suddenly I looked away from the
ceiling, there, lying there on my back on
my bed which had been your bed when my

bedroom was your bedroom and I stared at
your old wallpaper and from way in me
a deep, deep having lost someone came up
through my throat. I knew! Suddenly one
afternoon in the year that I was fourteen
that you wouldn't ever come back to me,
Mother—Big Billy always took us to visit
where they say you lie, on your birthdays,
then take Young Billy and me out to eat—
—so in this celebrating of your birthday
you were always visualized, never forgotten,

I'll give Big Billy that, he did love you
within his illness, his perpetual blessing
himself when he wasn't wiping yukky runny
fried egg from his "I must be appeased" chin
frothing, always frothing, raging at how life

had outwitted him the time he snuck you away
Mother from the family Christmas sing-around-
the-piano when he had come with my aunt who
thought she was going to marry him until I
materialized in you, Mother, but Big Billy did
love you, it fitted his romance, the one about

how God took you from him because of what he
did, Mamma!—He foisted all his professed
love of any child of his upon Young Billy who
needed love, too, and found himself doing just
about anything Big Billy seemed to want him to,
until, finally, I never saw a man absolutely
hate even the memory of his father the way
Young Billy hates Big Billy because to have
Big Billy's love, Young Billy had to give his
very personality, it's a wonder he survived!
Thank God, he did, Mother, Young Billy did

survive and you can be proud of him, Mother—
What slop!, soap opera!— It's "American," though,
and absolutely true . . . We are a nation in our
adolescence, still, over two hundred years old!
Our enemies go crazy that we survive in our
cherubic simplistic idiocy . . . Mother, I would
look at your name chiseled in stone and not
believe it . . . You were really away taking care
of a . . . I wanted you so much, Mother. You
weren't in that earth, Big Billy kept taking me
to and showing me . . . but suddenly I knew you

really were, Mother! . . . One afternoon in the
year that I was fourteen I knew that you were
dead. But I couldn't say it, even whisper, even
in a whisper to myself. I couldn't say it . . . You

were dead, not just away, but gone, oh, God!
so I am trying to write you a trilogy, to leave
something of us on this earth when I too breathe
no more, a trilogy, Mother, of flesh and bleeding,
not always pretty, and I was not always the good
boy I have always believed you asked me to be,
there are those who would tell you that I am not

now a real man, that I have never been a real man
and that I will never be a real man. I know I am
broken, but a coward, no, Mother. I would die as
well as most do, which is not very well. Why, I
might even be Nathan Hale on a scaffold but
won't seek one to prove it, thank you! Who
knows until their final minute shines how
they'll go out? . . . I am the best and the least
of mankind . . . but, Mother, I am the struggler
and survivor you made me cuddled in your arms.
Now what I become lies in me . . . And Father,

you and I must find each other . . . this little
country that became vast, where common men got
told for the first time in rememberable history
they had a right to the pursuit of happiness
and have not been able to handle it . . . Greed
always takes purity's place. American: He made
a motor to pull four wheels faster than two
hundred horses—beat gravity after eons lifting
flying tons into the sky and even through
very Heaven . . . He is even able to obliterate his
very trace and this earth burned-out ball float

forever as if ideas and lust and dreams
and desire never existed and no one left
to see where the burned-out ball goes

frighteningly floating . . . Now, Boppledock,
your son, Father, wanders vague through living,
drinking at success, risking freedom . . . every
once in a while a shudder of recall through him . . .

. . . once he went up to take a race
in Cummington . . . he come outa th'service, see,
and was down at th'V.A. when he picks up this
book a'po'try . . . it'd been squeezed,
crumbled up some pocket "Walkin' t'Sleep" or
sumthin' . . . by somebody named Wilbur . . . and he
"thought" he seen John Wayne tellin' Ward Bond
what to do so he went up there, you know, once more
to find the original dream, to run, fight
some Kelly, Kelley? . . . was th'opponent's
name Kelley!? . . . but it never happened, it
was all just a poem . . . who reads poems . . . he
couldn't make Comanches for John Wayne to
shoot the eyes out of so they'd have to

wander between th'four winds forever and
never see God, even in his head, like horror
hangover, this Kelley, Kelly? this runner
come down Dodwells Road and beat him . . . everything
beat Boppledock . . . Father . . . my Father . . . I,
your son, Boppledock was born in the dawn of
Margarine, old tires lying like lifesavers
all over front yards, scraggly grass strangled
in mud and cars with parts missing up on
blocks rusting. Even the breathing were dead in
their futility . . . Boppledock, Depression Era baby,

son of Mom and Dad who flapped their way through
th'20s like money would never end and when it
did in bleak 30s all opportunity took a walk

to war plants ten years down the road of selling
the seat off your own toilet door-to-door for
bread in poor man's gravy made out of flour in
bubbling water in hot pan with grease. It was the
dawn of Margarine, white like lard,
disgusting looking with a little
bag of yellow color that you mixed
and mixed and told yourself tasted

like butter . . . Lucky to have it. The
air was mean . . . Father, I am your son,
Boppledock, and I will tell you I love you
when we meet . . . I didn't do any better
than you with all my complaining, all
my forever everything's your fault, never
does there ever seem to come a point
where it is my fault not your fault!
Father, I have whined myself out of whining.
Failure, finally, is our own fault, it was
never really your fault, Dad, except for

being dumb of my child abuse . . . yet all
experience turns on kinds of insights one might
never have otherwise. Who knows what's "good" or
"bad" . . . the sheltered who cannot function once
Mother and Dad vanish or the abused who can never
hold anyone close, feel warmth, give love? I know
this—we have a country, my Father, that was hard
won by common men and must not be taken by the
rich from us . . . I cannot say to you, my Father,
provider of my three meals every day
and my bed every day and Christmas

every year for almost twenty years
that I do not love you. I yearn for

my own child's love. What can I say
to you . . . ! I was Depression Era baby
born when money would never end and
when it did . . . young nineteen-year-old
Housekeeper, underpaid by stingy Dad
who blessed himself as if that forgave it.
Nobody else had to live, though, Father
you were one of the very few who could
hire anyone when mother died leaving me

to nineteen-year-old Housekeeper just
growing up out of terror of spanked childhood
herself, now raged her vengeance for being
abused on *you*, Boppledock, middle-age drunk . . .
wandering in a sea of Guinness Stout out of
Little Hope . . . she had your pants down as
often as look at you, maybe thrilled by
your humiliation with lust become mean nasty
erotic to make your bare bottom red for what
she had to do across automobile front seats,
dodging the stiff stick shift to get a boy to

take her dancing and he'd put his boot
up you quick as look at you if you
so much as looked at him as you asked his
Sunday afternoon blowjob for something
to eat. He'd come to see her with nothing
better to do and for ego relief that
something of his worked in these times,
getting her with his flesh for a
woman putting him on earth, he almost
guaranteed your ass would pay for it,
throttling her life hole with his lifegiver

was better than kicking tin cans down

a dirt road or standing around some car
with its rod thrown, angry he couldn't
make it drive. He most likely walked into
auto-tire-strewn yard, bleak, lonely, awful in
its hot destitute silence . . . hot without money.
No Television then. Hot sun in no noise . . . except
maybe far off a radio singing Ruth Etting . . . Hot
day seeming to take forever to end and become
nightmare night into day never coming to an
end and you Boppledock's been stuck on her to

watch, only a brutalized child herself, a "girl" at
that, not "important," not her father's son! A girl
he'd ruined. One day in, say, late April when she
was just a little girl, she did something like
come down to breakfast late, or she
didn't get home from school on time or
left dirty clothes all over her
room and "Old Stonington" th'Sea Captain her
father, yanked her like a Raggedy Ann to
front parlor window and forced her to look
across street at Fire Chief Marston's

house while Sea Captain, "Old Stonington,"
her father, told her that when the Circus
came to town in July, he wouldn't take
her he'd take Fire Chief Marston's
little girl and all Spring passed
in its sweet smells while she
hoped against sinking-heart dread
that he didn't mean it but to Sea Captain,
"Old Stonington" this cruelty would "make"
a woman out of her, hard and knowing what
life's like . . . was better than having to

———

order her four hundred lashes for
disobeying him until she was split-skinned
dead and he'd have to go round steely-eyed
staring straight ahead, nobly concealing
his sorrow . . . he was what they call a
good man according to his lights and in July
when the clowns came for little children's hearts,
Sea Captain, "Old Stonington, Connecticut," her
father, kept his word . . . So young Housekeeper
she turned cold to any other child's cry,
in fact inflicted it . . . and actually expected

30 years later, Boppledock would, as an
adult, accept her explanation of how she
almost turned him stalker, unable to ever
hold anyone close, robbed of joy, life
happiness of personal involvement with
anyone or anything but bare survival, lost,
dumped through depression years into slaughter . . .
she, a "girl" screamed at to bring her father,
"Old Stonington," Sea Captain his hot bisquits
and baked beans while her brothers and everyone
beamed what a good idea it was she could take

dead mother's place, cooking, washing, waiting
on Pa every way but in bed; she had a prick to
deal with every way you look at it, kicked out by
"Old Stonington," Sea Captain, her father to baby-sit
for whatever she could get . . . into the great American
Depression. The air was mean. Children were to be "seen"
and not "heard." It was a miracle anyone ever
grew up . . . But Father, our final binding
love is I am mingled with your unfulfilled
wish to become again the original and to
make a future, your wildest imagining!

Book Three:

The

Clear

Blue

Lobster-Water

Country

I

   . . . Bop's thoughts spinning in
shot flashes . . . Central America's
America t'be in, Bop tried

to reassure himself now lying near
buzz of voices . . . Father . . . Bop
. . . vaporized!?

Mrs. Bop's face
embossed on some
clinging cliff?

Charred skin hanging off bones,
eyes hanging out . . . Lollibop
melted among roaches . . .

     . . . our dead parents' voices
come out of our mouths . . .
. . . Lolli, I wish

I'd spent more time
with you . . . am I like Big Billy, was
he like The O'Dock . . .?

My Grandfather, Michael The O'Dock,
rushed with his hand clutched
in his mother's to escape

potatoes grinning black in their cores
and the Irish walking dead in their
own land. Dole or work

never come for those who counted
on a life of spuds. It was to
America The O'Dock came.

Again the sea spews
barely believing humans
for America's one more chance.

These new among us
busy finding roof,
food, new start

are not oblivious to
possible pop that
would boil the ocean,

think of it! Glutton lobster
sneakin' along to sit on
some Mussel to eat it gulping

cooking right there in its own
seaweed, right there turning
orange in its bubbles

not up outa trap into
steamin' pot but
in its own sea.

Life's breath snuffed, cold, even
th'Moon gone, teeth chattering
in your broiled skull.

II

I was over to th'university because

Lollibop told me I ought t'learn more
'bout different worlds, not

be a Boppledock all m'life! . . . though
jest what she means by that I
couldn't figure . . . I went

t'th'university-n-met fine people
who work with *Hands Off Central America*
-n-I went over to th'university

to learn 'bout other countries without
ever bein' in any a'them, it's maybe
called fightin' f'freedom from afar . . .

They hold meetings, protest, bring
Ireland-n-Central America to my
attention in my mailbox . . . but

this Joe Strange, teaches a course
in how to speak English-n-act human, he
says to me th'world's become selfish.

Joe says that down in Central America, soldiers,
dictators, death squads; Joe said to me, Father,
I could do alot jest goin' with him onna

short trip with some help, let 'em
see all Americans aren't their
common man's enemy . . . Joe

said, Father, somethin'
like my goin' with him would be
somethin' with nuthin' visible

in it for me. 'Course we could git slabbed, I
think what I'm tryin' to tell you, Father,
is I think I see my life's need-n-I

put all this down f'you
now th'rest is for
old Boppledock.

III

Here in green life old truck
carrying American aid bounces
Boppledock and Joe Strange like pancakes

flip over up and down on their seats
traveling mud ruts. It is like
meadows of Custer . . .

Boppledock Sixty-Six
at least in real action,
now in it, the

bullets throw him out of truck and smack
him on his back. Joe Strange behind
steering wheel when the picture

goes out of his eyes, looking
for it through windshield. Bop aware
that several are taking what is in truck

and vanishing like he wasn't lying
there. No one comes to fire
bullet into his head, these

are peasants, it is a shrug.
If he can manage to live
alright! . . .

IV

. . . In the tiny little bit of Ireland
my Grandfather, The O'Dock, ever saw
as a little child in dust's death

never did he see a black man. Come here to
America he and his mother hardly found
any blacks even on a clear blue lobster-water

country side street . . . People weren't
outside their ghettos mingling in among
the white Protestants, trying to

could cost you your life in clear blue
lobster-water country ignorance,
cruelty, bullying, forcing anyone

you found frightening to do vile things
in lobster frustration, always gettin'
up early cold-n-workin' wind cold

sea slappin' you like a snaked belt buckle
until your joints seized up before you
were even forty, there wasn't much in

your life, not even radio then, hardly any
blacks either in the clear blue lobster-
water country . . . "too cold f'em-n-they like

sugar-n-hot places!" Maybe one. One tall one,
maybe one lean one down at th'sardine factory, who know
why he come s'far up north where th'green

in th'Pines is always blood deep
green-n-th'cold never really
goes away even onna bright hot

orange lobster stew day when
th'clouds in th'sky look like
butter in milk-n-all th'tourists

in their purple shorts-n-flappy hats are
thinkin' 'bout swimmin' mebbe drivin'
over t'Old Orchard where you could git in

by Googins' rocks-n-it's pretty warm but
always th'chill never leaves, why a black man
even thought he could escape whatever overwhelmin'

Harlem he run frum witha woman-n-two little-uns,
what'ud he think would be better here . . . mebbe
jest livin' in among faces of other colors . . .

. . . Now thet don' seem like thet 'ud be hit!
Whut could hit be!? One lean black at
th'sardine factory who stood out so

y'didn't have t'look very hard t'find where
he lived, collapsin' brick inside which
a couple a'wide-eyed innocent black faces and a

woman impassive lest an expression from her
git them killed or evicted-n-Colon Foocum he say
he ain'na gonna wuk with no . . . but Mr. Ross a'Ross Sardines say

yessir he gonna 'cause th'powerful young black
ten times th'wukker any one a you is—seems
this man wants his job t'feed his family, so,

Colon Foocum git th'boys-n-
they show this black some goo-ud lobster fun
yesindeedie! Ayuh I know hit! until it whispered

up-n-down th'wharfs you could play with this black.
Have you fun! . . . you could play with this un he
want his job s'bad in rubber apron an' boots, in

th'rubber people who wuk with fish all th'time gettin'
hosed of fish scales wear-n- it was
whispered in snicker that he had a dong

on him he could git all th'way up a'elephant,
yesireebob! He'd show it t'you 'f you told him
he might not be needed no more at th'sardine

factory-n-some a'th'boys led by Colon Foocum'ud
git him out back-n-taken theirn out-a-make
him take his out-n-git on his

knees-n-put theirn in 'is mouth while
he jerkin' thet big thing a'hissen
like Colon tell him—then

they'd tell him they like th'dark meat of fish
out back a'th'sardine factory on th'rickety
little platform, hidden, with nuthin' but

lobsters t'see 'f they wanna-n-th'men
several who go t'church Sundays-n-always
turn out th'light never lettin' even their wives

ever see theirn, gathered roun' t'watch,
they wouldn't none a'them taken theirn out-n-have
Colon Foocum ever able t'say

they had theirn right out 'long withhissen-goo-ud
Christian hardwukkin' God-fishin' fellas from
th'isolation called futility . . . Colon he say

no furrener better think he cummin' inta th'clear
blue lobster-water country-n-take a payday
frum any real American like th'Foocums since

they took th'handcuffs offa Fester Foocum
inna earliest settlin', they only
so many fish-n-so many jobs . . . ayuh I know hit!

V

. . . No longer Ellis Island, my Father,
but on toothpicks with sails
sinking all the way from Cambodia

and in boats impossible to float
from Vietnam, the sea permits
them to beach on America . . .

. . . Just last week these
were eating field mice in their squeals
for fresh warm life-sustaining

live blood and protein . . . Now
entering my America, my culture
through Los Angeles, here,

Father, is where San Salvador is now
if San Salvador can get here! This rush
from death can suffocate

you and me become
Coca-Cola Home Fries soft
on the evening of the

Mushroom taking our last blinding
picture like Christ rising from the dead.
You have shown us how You did it, God, enough!

Father, to survive
we must hunger like these
rice-paddy skeletons

come now desiring
your lust, your
open door.

      . . . Lying here Boppledock sees
      Mrs. Bop in that flash we all
      suffer, flash of going down . . .

Once I would have caught your breath for you!
What lasts longer, the knotty thick tree
or fleeting wildflower that stirs

your blood but wilts? Come, lady,
let me stick my sword in you hard
and pulsing my life, whispering

I love you in your acorn hair still
fresh from country hay and lust. Soon
it could be you, my love, looking

a splashed pumpkin grin cut
that holds my heart. Oh I have looked
like death, lady, for a long time now

layers of age over youth, glass windows
over eyes desiring. We become good-looking
as we near permanence . . .

"There, easy now!"
He was hearing words,
Boppledock realized.

"You've got luck!" a grinning
accordion jello face
was moving the words

into Boppledock's hearing
like that wish we all have to
come back from our graves granted.

"Your pal, identification says
Joe Strange, looks like he's
looking at some centerfold."

"Joe's alright?" Boppledock
tried to move but seemed
held down though nothing held him.

"Easy—you're hit . . . no, your
Strange friend took it neat
right in the center of his forehead

but the strange thing is his look is
as if he got answers, it's fine
with him!" This accordion jello face

seemed surrounded by other men who looked
just like the men who shot him. "It's
tragic, Mr. Dock. We got here from

Headquarters Command in time to tell these
gentlemen that you're on their side.
They find it hard to know which

Americans are which."
—"That's th'world today" . . . Boppledock
dozed . . . Father, I tried

to be a part of it and almost got slabbed but
it's better to go home and sit on my stoop knowing
it's not th'barstool of a loser it's

my front porch
that I took my chances for, my
share of this earth, Father . . .

        . . . Bop suddenly was aware that
        everything was dead silence now
        here where he lay on a stretcher in

        Central America, turning his head he
        didn't turn it far . . . There, just on
        the rim of his left eye, directly into it

        as he turned his head was the hole
        of an automatic pointed right at him
        by one of the young guerrillas . . . it

        was like enemy were passing them close
        so near they dared not make sound and
        if Bop did, even accidentally, even if he

couldn't control a sneeze, the way
we can't sometimes, especially times that
embarrass us, when somebody is speaking or

a magician performing and our sneeze breaks
everyone's concentration . . . but if Bop
breathed, so much as shifted his

uncomfortable position and anything
happened, shooting started, they all
had to run, the young guerrilla

would black out Bop in orange forever . . . he
was without expression, his eyes cat's-
eye marble, he and Bop waiting for danger to go.

VI

An ale of sea filled Bop's head, now,
memory, like an overwhelming wave
large like a tongue, to smash a beach . . .

. . . Bop, facing, suddenly, lying here
in Central America . . . I had to run
outa th'clear blue lobster-water country where

th'deep soul heart of me is, rush outa there from
frightened people, savage in their frustration,
over me in deep depression kickin'

you quick outa th'way more than
ever takin' care a'you, a plate
of cold food, Franco-American Spaghetti

outa a can opened fast-n-thrown at you

with a snarl-n-you better not complain
or ask for seconds, or you'd go

right to bed without anything! Meanness
is from nothing you ever do
bringing you happiness . . .

. . . Th'sea never pays well, it makes you
into th'froth of its waves . . . Th'lobster ocean
is loud, you have to speak up, your

opportunity can be drowned. Jimmy Economo
yelled loud! He talked loud, you could hear
Jim Economo loud wherever he

was, in Luke's Coffee Pot next to
Chuck's Clothes, especially in his office.
You could hear Jim way out in th'middle

of th'street, you'd think folks wuz
deaf th'loud way Jim Economo said anything!
Jim, second-generation Greek in a

silent, quiet Protestant New England, become
a big lawyer, District Attorney, though
they always sent some climber from

th'Prosecutor's office over t'Augusta if
a case wuz anythin' goo-ud, worthwhile, a
murder a'suthin' like 'at, goo-ud-Jimmy

Economo'd never git them! They
coulda made him celebrated,
t'warn't no one gonna let a Greek

shoeshine boy have suthin' like 'at no sir rebob!
Jimmy Economo was a success in a trap. This was
Protestant clear blue-n-don' no one wanna forgit it.

VII

Lime City has become hamburger stands now
and unskilled crime committed
from despair's overwhelming fatigue,

ignorance's inability to do better, crimes
dangerous only by accident, you're liable
t'git hurt 'f you suddenly come upon

someone in th'process a'tryin' t'take
th'stereo outa y'car . . . th'old-timers
used t'gettin' by on nothin' yet

somehow with enough-n-retired,
can't explain it to themselves, what
are dreams 'f you can't afford 'em . . . still

the sea blood blue some days and
sharp in your nose, sea smell clear clean
with the death of the sardine on its breath

like the stench in the air in paper mill towns
mingled with lobster fresh salt sea air
smell of lobsters thrust up in their traps, seaweed

clinging like strangling podded ropes though
their own greed, as all ours,
predicts their end . . . and in

traps set down where they crawl with all their

tufted spindle legs, feelers on anything
to eat until it is us who will eat them.

In lobster towns the silence
of death as a business keeps faces'
lips tight without knowing why, maybe.

Maybe we don't know why! The sea is grim
when you reach in her until you have scooped her out,
taken all her lobster forever.

VIII

"We all tried to get Jim Economo to listen, to
hear us!" Attorney-at-law Young Billy Dock said
to his brother, Bop,

sitting at a hotel dining room table,
looking out on ocean, clear blue lobster-
water blue, blue-green, Sea Gull splashed

and lobsters, moving devouring garbage cans
of the sea, eating everything along
the shook seafloor . . . which

makes their sweet meat, death makes
food for life . . . Bop reminisced,
"Jimmy Economo shined shoes all his boyhood."

"Specifically, what are you saying!?" Young Billy
asked, thinly veiling exasperation . . .
. . . "Until," Bop finished,

"he almost developed a permanent subservient hump
from bending over shoes to snap a shine
on them, and he walked around spittoons

with an apron on with pockets to put nickels
in he collected from Pool players, dropping
nickels into the apron pockets along with

shoeshine money, finally he burst out
of it to law school . . ."
"We advised Jimmy that our considered opinion was

not to get Savas out of Augusta
State Hospital." Young Billy
started again . . . Bop interrupted, "Jimmy insisted?"

Young Billy picked up his drink and said,
"Wouldn't listen. You know how loud
Jim Economo can be!" . . . Bop, carefully,

"He was rising above th'pool tables . . ." Young Billy
looked at Bop as he might at a witness, or someone he was
certain was guilty, but, nevertheless, would represent . . .

"Well," Young Billy continued, "much against our
good counsel, Jim Economo brought his client, Savas,
here and took him into his office."

"Don't tell me," Bop blurted, "Jim got lobster-grabbed!"
"Yes," Young Billy looked momentarily amused, "that's
exactly it, all hell broke loose, as you

put it, lobster claw pinched good! When they got inside
Jimmy Economo's office and Jimmy had Savas sat down
to listen to his wisdom, Savas shot him five times."

IX

It was always vague exactly where

Paul Economo came from to the
clear blue lobster-water country . . . he

was a wonder! A wonder and a worker!
He started a shoeshine stand-n-added
a poolroom right across from Mae's Ice Cream

Parlor. Fishermen came in with
sea stink in their clothes, stomach-
wrenching smell of fish and relit cold cigars,

while Paul Economo, then
Paul Economo-n-his four boys,
walked around collecting nickels for pool games

and shined shoes. Big Billy, Smilin' Billy,
forbade Bop to ever go in there while
he'd stop outside, make a point

of stopping on Main Street, right out there publicly
on Main Street where word of who wuz speakin' t'who
spread up-n-down Main Street from one end t'other;

Big Smilin' Billy outside Paul Economo's
where he could be plainly seen talkin' to
Paul Economo, yesindeedie, ayuh, I know hit-n-Paul

Economo beaming, Big Billy smilin' that
Smilin' Billy smile a'hisen, chattin' affably
with Paul Economo beaming at talking with

one a'th'white chosen, who, while not Protestant but
Irish, even Catholic!—was quality worth talkin' to in
that New England town, telling everyone,

Big Billy telling everyone what a
hard worker and good man Paul Economo was but
forbidding Bop ever to go in Paul's, which in

Big Billy's I must be appeased imagination
never needed checking on all the years
Boppledock was in Paul's every day being

welcome for his nickels while looked at with
contempt as spoiled, no account . . . Young
Billy Dock wuz what any Pool shark-ud want

a boy a'his t'be like . . . one by one the sons
of Paul Economo left the Lime City where
old Paul had hoped they'd settle,

Ralph, to Rhode Island, nuthin' more-n-a truck driver,
Joe, to th'Merchant Marine, never wrote, Bobby, th'glamour boy
driftin' America a Golf bum . . . but Jimmy,

Jimmy to law school, Paul Economo's pride,
shot for trying to help
one of their own . . .

        . . . Bop told Young Billy he'd be right back,
        got up and walked out of Young Billy's
        sight for a few minutes, as if he

        was going to the men's room, making a
        phone call, suddenly sitting there had
        become overwhelming, he could see

        Jimmy Economo, a boy, times after school
        Bop'ud come into Paul's with snow, brushing off
        snowflakes, Jimmy smiling, proud, no

submission, in fact an arrogance in
the way he'd shine shoes, and he looked
like a wise owl coming from collecting

in the poolroom, like he saw his university,
his law school in the jingling change in
his pockets . . . Once, when the Athletic

Coach at Lime City High School was
threatened with losing his job, Peggy
Croft, of The Crofts, told Bop if he

and that Jimmy Economo didn't stay
out of it, stop going round getting
signed student petitions protesting

the Coach's dismissal, their names
would be mud in Lime City, but that
made Big Billy furious that even a Croft

would dare say to a Dock, now, these
days, that he couldn't stand up for
an Athletic Coach, Poetry'ud be

somethin' else, but anybody gifted at
teachin' how to round third-n-spike goo-ud
oughta be stood up for, so with

Big Billy approving, which delighted
Paul Economo, that a son of his was
exercising democracy with th'son of

a real American, Jim and Bop, Bop and
Jim, were close for a minute, exercising
principle and ethics, and saved th'Coach's

job, then fell apart back into
their positions, but Bop
never forgot the expression

of Greek democratic fierce
pride in Jimmy Economo's
look . . .

X

. . . Again now, Young Billy signaled
for another drink . . . "A couple of years ago,"
he began again, "This Greek like

Jim Economo's Greek . . ." Bop nodded,
"This Savas got angry at some lawyer
over around Bangor, kept insisting

the lawyer cheated him and he shot him."
"What they do?" Young Billy waved
to the waiter again . . . "They prosecuted . . . Open-

and-shut case! Any Prosecutor, ANY Prosecutor
would love it!!" Their drinks arrived . . . Outside
against the lobster sky, tired lobstermen

started in with the day's haul. The weather cold
clean sharp sea salt wind on the clear blue . . . Young
Billy commented, "He, Savas, got declared

insane."—Young Billy's features took on
a stern disapproval, as he
said, "He didn't wound that first lawyer badly."

"That . . . first lawyer!!?" Bop was taken aback!

Young Billy looked hard at Bop.
"Yep, that first lawyer! Well after about

eight months in Augusta State Hospital another
lawyer gets Savas a pass, how he did it or why,
don't ask me. He's out! He goes to see the

lawyer who just loosed him back among us after
nearly a year and he shoots him too!" Bop
intentionally looked aghast, allowing

Young Billy to have his I must be appeased
attention so he'd continue, not frown, not
recede within himself in the sulk of drinking

convinced Bop wasn't listening to his show, his
obviously insightful description, he imagined.
—"Well, our Jim Economo, second-generation

Greek from Poolroom to D.A. to
Private Practice, good-hearted Jim Economo wasn't
going to have it said of him in the

Lime City he grew up in of the
clear blue lobster-water country, that a
countryman of his could have trouble and

be alone, no sir! no sir rebob! Jim
Economo, all Paul Economo has left except
his girls, his daughters." Young Billy stopped,

as if he had finished a summation . . . Yeah, his
girls, Bop realized, Paul Economo's got girls but
he wouldn't think girls matter! Bop said now,

"Jim Economo stepped up out of shoeshining
to walk with Protestants and eat th'same
lobster they do . . ." Bop shook his head and said, "Jim

jest couldn't resist tryin' to shove
a little wiseass at whispering Protestants
who would keep him stooped shining shoes his

whole life if they could . . . if it wasn't
for his immigrant father, a wonder,
and for his own hard hard work in law school, to give

the clear blue lobster-water country Protestants a
message, loud, that we Greeks are together!"
"Guess what!?" Young Billy said, "He decided to

represent Savas . . . worse." Bop waited.
Young Billy went on, "The first
thing he did was to tell this Savas, his

client, that he'll get him out of the
State hospital." . . . "I can't believe this!" Bop
squirmed around in his chair. Lips pursed,

Young Billy said, "Those of us who practice
law pointed out to Jim Economo that
Savas's aim was getting better, but you

couldn't get Jim to listen. Savas was his client
and, as important, unable to speak good English and
nobody was going to keep a Jimmy Economo

client locked up awaiting proceedings."
"How," asked Bop, shaking his head . . . "How,
under any stretch of anybody's imagination,

did Savas become bailable!?" "Who knows!?"
Young Billy mused and grinned as if
privately enjoying lawyer ability . . . "That's

what lawyers are around for, to do the
impossible!" Young Billy sucked his glass.
The smooth hoochino was beginning

to make him look preserved. "I guess
when he got to the point where psychiatrists
thought him well enough to issue a pass so he

could confer with the second lawyer about
shooting and wounding the first lawyer, I
guess that somehow, technically, even though he

shot his second lawyer, too, and was now answerable
for two shootings, I guess, somehow, being able to
get a pass got him to some weird status where

Jim Economo could get him out on bail, if he
could post it." "Humanity backfired on Jim," Bop
commented. Young Billy looked at Bop waiting . . .

"Trying to be compassionate," Bop finished, "to
raise another immigrant to the treatment a white
Protestant would expect, got Jim Economo shot."

They could see lobstermen
far away now toward their
beaches, tired, the death of the day

ready to be sorted on rough piers,
wharves that looked rickety in tar gravel
and the lobster gone out of the Penobscot forever.

Bop said, "Think, Young Billy . . . all Jimmy
Economo's hard hard work, everything went
out the bullet holes in him." "No, he's

recovering," Young Billy stated. They both would
leave the Lime City Hotel dining room now and
outside on the sidewalk, part, Young Billy fast.

Holding the hotel door open for them, Bop mused,
"Somehow, I don't think anybody could be
th'same after somebody shot you." . . . Walking by

himself up Main Street past Paul Economo's
Pool Parlor, shoeshine business, Bop tried
to fantasize his Father, to see Big Billy,

Smilin' Billy standing, talking there . . . right
there!! . . . with Paul Economo . . . instead Jimmy
Economo filled his mind, he could hear the shots.

. . . The first bullet, Jim's arms become like
snapped twigs that, muscled, rippled snapping
shines on shoes . . . and bullet two took his

body's generated strength to lift him above it all.
Shot three canned his ambition in his wounds, and
after shot four, all his heart's lust

out the sieve of him . . . the fifth bullet
made certain he must always admit a
companion to his privacy . . .

XI

My Grandfather, Michael The O'Dock,

from County Clare, Ireland,
ordered a house to be built of granite

in Portland, Maine, of the clear blue
lobster-water country. It is war awful
to have your old home bombed to a wall

staggering in its sweat, a sliver of ghosts,
but as bad to have the house your Grandfather
ordered built still there but lived in by

strangers because in America whole families
made believe they were who they weren't, the
immigrant foolishly proud to brag

that no child of his would ever
have to do what he had to do, have to know
what one who is transplanted must survive,

suffer, in order to get a house
and education for his children in the
colleges; but no instinct who they

really were: nobodies because they
had no real money under them always
in eviction's shadow . . . and hidden

in among them, frantic masses
coming to America, potential
assassins with no apparent grudge.

XII

    . . . Now breezes on Bop's face, like
    licking tongues, lying here
    on a stretcher, the inside head's

razor-slicing memory—Mrs. Bop and
Lollibop came with me t'New York
as I left f'here . . .

They were suddenly frantic at
m'sudden goin' as underneath all
th'bitchin' was love . . . They were

scared, intuition feared we all
would never see each other again . . .
. . . M'sudden goin', comin' here

to my life, at last participatin',
at last inna world I sidestepped
swillin' ale-n-excuses . . . arrivin'

in New York . . . "Wanna cab," drenching
downpour, grab your suitcases; in
The Drake lobby, hidden in the cubicle

where you buy newspapers, Bop
suddenly saw Lollibop being cruised
by a smooth Dutch young man and when

she smiled her baby look suddenly
peeked through her 28-year-
old flush of happy youth being approached,

and they were walking over to the
lobby bar opposite the elevators as
Bop crossed the lobby and went up to be with

Mrs. Bop who had made his whole life valuable,
even when sunk in drink he could not but
fail her and now going off to Central

America on her, in order to be
part of life he had been so broken in
childhood as to be unable to get into

anything, he was now, again, abandoning
her . . . What is it that makes us
think we'll find everything

anywhere else than where
it's always been, in the arms of our love
and our children, but we do! We always

do it, run to look where nothing is, what
is it in us that breaks the hearts
of the only people who love us? Robbed of

our mother's cradling, a never-filled
loss, and we cannot seem to stop ourselves
from abandoning what we have! Loved ones, life

with them, their love of us, yet we seek as if
we feel we are violated out of our share
of . . . What!!?, while we give

everyone else smiles, our charm acting
as we think we are expected
to with everyone who doesn't matter . . . Just

. . . then . . . now lying here on
Central American ground, hurt, the face of
Smilin' Billy, of Big Billy, filled Bop's

head and the old ache back, spraining his
nerves so they were like a thousand ants
having their feast of him . . . Fa-ther . . . in

Bop's . . . thoughts—Fa-ther, this fat little
gray man with th'potbelly snout . . . is . . .
Lahty! . . . FATHER, it's Lahty! NOW, Father

. . . tell me that you love me . . . now . . .
. . . Pressure like fingers reaching for
him slipping, Bop seeming to slip out of

the fingers' grasp of something, as if
he was something becoming slippery to
something trying to take hold of him . . . then

as suddenly he felt alright, the
frightening was gone . . . Bop raised
himself up a bit now, all around

him the guerrillas were coming and going, it
seemed aimlessly, they didn't seem
to really be going anywhere, yet,

Bop realized they knew what
they were about . . . They're
tryin' t'do here what

we come to America t'do, Bop
fumbled with it . . . like
. . . m'Grandfather, like

Michael The O'Dock, my Grandfather . . . rushing
to America with his hand clutched
in his mother's . . .

XIII

All Michael The O'Dock did in America

is almost vanished; there are not
even Headstones with the names

of his children on them in the
South Portland, Maine, graveyard, and not one of them
would have a plot to lie in either if Michael

The O'Dock hadn't himself bought enough land
to hold eleven of his thirteen children and
his mother and his wife and himself forever in

South Portland, Maine, of the clear blue lobster-
water country. None of my Grandfather Michael
The O'Dock's daughters have headstones with

their names on them over their graves.
It is as if they were all stillborn but
they weren't and lived to be old.

XIV

Accordion jello face came over
and got down on his haunches
by Boppledock.

"How you feeling?" his leathered
face was like it had been slashed deep
by knuckles of razors but it hadn't,

years of serving under the sun
and weather made the face give
where it had to, lines allowing

the skin to stay in one piece.
"I don' know how I feel!" Bop replied
hardly sorry at his irritability . . .

"Can I get you something we got?"
"No thanks." Bop suddenly looked at him.—
"You're not Spanish?" "No I'm

part of the U.S. Army that's here
jes' visitin'." He grinned. "I came
here to look," Bop said, "to see

if I could help little people get
to vote, pick their system." Accordion
jello face tried to hide his

opinion of that but couldn't mask
his look. Bop asked, "Do you think we
ought to come here for Dictators?"

Accordion jello face put his palms up.
"I'm jes' a soldier, if I live through it,
jes' live through this right here, I get

out! Master Sergeant Alfred Kelly is
out, through!!" Bop looked up at him so
hard he felt like he'd wrenched his

neck. "Kelly!?" "That's th'name!"
. . . Bop scowled . . . "There's always so
many Kellys, never th'right one!" Bop

let himself down to lie flatter . . . "You
been lookin' for somebody named Kelly, I'll
ask around, I m'se'f didn't know

they wuz another Kelly out here with us . . .
What's th'Kelly you want's first name?"
"I never knew" Bop drifted . . . Master

Sergeant Alfred Kelly stood up, in the
uncertain way of the confused who

can't be sure just what you're saying to
them, he shrugged, shot a wave of his hand at
Bop and walked off . . . Just then home

overwhelmed Bop's thoughts . . . the waste of
lobster until they'll all be gone. Eaten by
farmers come in from their

planting, themselves grown a part
of their crops; lobstermen bent at
their hauling dead weight from deep

ocean, crustacean ignorant
of their scavenging: lobster
ravished off their rocks to

feed selfishness not necessity, and
tourists eating them to feel they're
getting something special for all the

hours of their drudgery, yet
unconsciously guilty, aware you don't
just go get lobster like you

pick an apple off a tree because
like cow udders bursting unmilked
you either pick the apple or

the tree throws it to earth for the pigs
or to rot, but lobsters would
continue living and crawling,

clearing the salt green sea
of its refuse if we didn't
drop traps for them.

XV

Father we'll
meet again.

You can tell me you love me then.

Mother, you have always been lost to me.
I hope there comes a time
when the game's over

and I can see you . . . life ends and you
become mine forever in among
you and those you always wished

to be with forever, your dead,
as you and Father are my never
forgotten dead, as my wife and I

will be our daughter's dead. Do
the dead all erase death
eternally together? What keeps

us without struggle and disappointment
if the dead do not erase death?
Now I'd like, Mother, to believe

the stupid struggle life is ends
and you become mine forever
in among you and those you always wished

to be with forever, your dead, as you
and Father are my never-forgotten dead . . . as
my wife and I will be our daughter's

dead . . . Do the dead all erase death? What
keeps us in some place called Heaven without
struggle and disappointment? . . . What do we do when

our excuses and blame are used up, gone, and there
we all are with each other . . .? Mother, would
it be better if we never met?

Is that what happens, yearning is only a device
to get us through this earth living until
we have earned whatever complicated

eternity is ours for our evil or our goodness but in it
there are no reunions, our life was our life
and while we are what we call alive

on this earth, we miss those who impregnated
and carried us—in our fright
of the unknown and our ignorance . . . Mother, Father,

I hope you are there when the Moon dips low
and I catch my ride . . . when the sweet scent
of Maine is just caught where my breath ends.

XVI

Baptized without choice when I was hardly born,
Confirmed into a religion I did not choose,
I was to break in terror of You and eternal damnation,

a toddler genuflecting and blessing myself or else!
"God will strike you dead if you do this!"
"God will strike you dead if you do that!" screeched

Big Billy who was afraid of God. So terrified
of You God, he was on his knees
when he needed to be up on his feet . . . I've

broken your most serious commandments, the ones
you never get to "see You" if you
do them; I've done that thing I

was taught I'd burn in Hell forever
if I did it, never ever see Your
face! . . . Let me say I'll

take whatever I've coming. I have faith
in You that Dante's Hell is Dante's need,
imagined pain becomes real pain in human need to

know a feeling that could get worse, and
makes possible reverent, fervent worship
of incomprehensible religion; people

close their eyes, moan and rock
thinking everyone knows what they're doing,
but most of all God knows so they'll

be saved in some Saturday afternoon
matinee Heaven with Lon McCallister and
June Haver in a lovely meadow green,

sunshine happy forever, forgetting that
here on earth we leave our paradisiacal
vacations worn out, tired of the beach,

weary of our last resort, back to rush and struggle,
but purity of motive is harder to achieve
than the hardest betrayal. Greed and neon

flickering death, anything to "get the order"—
Like Roman Church allowing Bop's friend Buffer Rose to
get his booze dollars hustlin' *La Catolica*

door to door flashing some imprimatur,
kept inside plastic against rain, that
has a picture of some Bishop in vestments

in the middle of the most important part of
The Mass, like giving Communion, a sight
certain to intimidate; Buffer Rose

with this imprimatur, like identification from God
Himself, sellin' magazine subscriptions by
terrifying poor guilty who do not dare

close their doors, once Buffer calls out,
knuckles pounding their locked doors,
"Th'church!" "Fa-ther sent me!"

"Saint Anthony, ma'm" . . . "San Antonio, Mamma!"
. . . and before they can open their mouths—"Who you
wanna Mass said for, y'Father, y'Mother . . .? It's

only Five ($5.00) for two years," Buffer
writin' th'order already as he speaks;
these people won't turn him away,

thinking of themselves, hoping
someone on earth will help pray them
finally into Heaven when they're not

on earth anymore where you can always
fall down on your knees and atone,
after they can't . . . half of each $5.00 order

is Buffer's, $1.25 to some vague Seminary
he uses in his pitch, "for poor boys who
wanna study for th'Priesthood"

he tells everyone; the Seminary prob'ly exists
and gets a trickle of quarters, just
barely keeping this legal . . . or the $1.25 each

order goes directly to Archdiocese, and $1.25
each order to shrewd hustler businessman,
Baldy Knox, who thought this up, said

to Father, "Can't harm anyone, gettin' a good
religious magazine-n-you will say th'Masses-n-
it'll get you cash from people who

don't come to Mass, so you'll never get their coin
in your collection basket" . . . Who . . . can prove it!?
Names, names, names of people's loved ones for whom

they've accepted another magazine into their house
in the resignation that at least Masses
are being said for someone they loved

to help them get into Heaven. Names
scribbled often quick by Buffer, maybe
not even written clearly if he's

movin' smooth, makin' sales-n-tryin'
t'hit as many doors as he can
before it rains or somebody calls th'Police . . . the

names handed to his sales crew chief, somebody
called Joe Egan or Mafia-soft low-key Vinnie Cura;

th'names of everyone who is to have
a Mass said for them, religiously
taken into Baldy Knox's office-n-Baldy Knox

lickin' his thumb thumbin' th'money . . .
Vinnie Cura explained to Buffer,
calmly, the day he joined them . . .

"We're doing them all such a
wonderful favor. They're guilty
poor people who don't have the

money to keep going out visiting
graveyards and it embarrasses them
to go to church Sundays with no

money to give, so, here we'll
take only $3.00 or $5.00 and
we make out, Baldy Knox makes out,

and they make out, know what I mean?
We tell them a Mass will be said for
those they can't afford, for their

Five dollars . . . They can afford it!"
Buffer, indignant, "Th'church, th'Seminary
gets money, too . . . n-th'Masses do

get said!!?" Vinnie Cura hissed,
"Of course they do," almost inaudibly . . . but
it bothered Buffer, who, like Bop,

had a lawyer brother, Atlee Rose,
staunch Catholic, never missed Mass,
went to Confession, Communion, prided himself

as head of claims for an insurance company, in
settling claims like where a woman had
lost both legs and sued for millions,

for Five Thousand out of court. She
couldn't wait, needed money, was
hungering for dollars; yet Atlee Rose

was calling Buffer a bilker of old ladies
for selling this *La Catolica* . . . It bothered
Buffer, Atlee must be right, must have

somethin' to do with education making what
Atlee Rose did to little people alright, but
Buffer wrong; f'example, who knows if

these names are ever given to a Priest to
say Masses, or if they are, if they're all then
not just dumped in a pile and one

Mass said, which in the goodness
and greatness of dear God is
supposed to be good enough? Who

would question that God didn't
see y'Father, y'Mother among a million
names hastily written by a

salesman moving fast while th'sun's shinin'? . . . and
. . . in America of The O'Dock from
County Clare, Ireland, Irish

committing sin certain to guarantee
your waiting a long time, if ever
you could get into Heaven out of

Purgatory or Limbo . . . brother
betraying brother for his own fresh start,
using education your own brother came to

America with his hand clutched in your mother's
and sweat to get you, to cheat him . . .
It was hunger that drove us out of Ireland,

still we could not see that when it came to it,
the church heavy on us had no miracle,
could not make potatoes where none

would grow anymore . . . Could not bless us luck
in strange savage lands, even if we
brought God along in our imagining . . .

XVII

My Grandfather, The O'Dock from
County Clare, Ireland, ordered a house
to be built of granite in Portland, Maine,

city of sardine stink and Burnham & Morrill
baked beans, oh it was elegant
for a self-made man to have his success

in America, what he accomplished from the
emigration from County Clare, Ireland, gone
forever from County Clare of his heart,

Clare of the sea and potato scabs, shadow

Ireland, land of starving and sure death if
you stayed. Jesus wouldn't make potatoes grow

f'all y'genuflectin' to Him and moanin' to
keep His broken faithful home
in His goodness and wisdom knowin'

what's best. He dispossessed the Irish.
. . . no one special because they're
Catholic or Protestant or anything a'tall a'tall.

XVIII

. . . My Grandfather, Michael The O'Dock,
ordered a house to be built of granite
in America, a good Irishman

who with his hand clutched in his mother's
came to this country on his childish guts
and staggered under luggage still a boy

as a baggage Porter in Portland, Maine,
railroad station until his mother, saving,
got enough for a grocery store, then five

and sending the money home to Ireland, educating
one brother a doctor, the other a lawyer and
bringing them over to America. My Grandfather,

The O'Dock, left a granite house behind him in
Portland, Maine, of the clear blue lobster-
water country, not gone to the grave with him

but still standing for me to almost come apart

looking at it because I can't go in it anymore . . . no.
We were Irish Catholic broken unable to

motivate to earn until too late to keep
my Grandfather's house! A house filled with great
frustration, my only brother Young Billy had to break

with me forever and that house and those people,
my aunts, the daughters of Michael The O'Dock
embalmed alive in the Irish religion, frightened,

terrorized tip your forelock Irish while saying
they weren't, insisting they weren't!, trembling in
gratitude for school teaching jobs in among

the Protestants of New England . . . wishing
to be thought Irish but a picture of Queen Victoria
in many Irish-American bathrooms, not ours, we

were green, aunts living out their whole
unmarried lives in the house their father
The O'Dock built for them, never remembering

a kind word from "Himself" or any gesture that
he loved them. They were the duty his dong
fulfilled for the church more than they ever

were his children in the house he ordered built
of granite four stories high if you counted the
dining room and kitchen sunk where

a cellar should be; grand staircases up from each
end of the hall but only the one in the back hall
going downstairs . . . then both winding staircases,

winding circular up and around like
a cardinal's capa magna unfolding up two floors to where
what would be anyone else's attic had three bedrooms

one of them with a skylight window we used to call "Tip Top,"
it was a grand house built for a wife and thirteen
children only the last a boy, Big Billy,

right across the street from Saint Dominic's
Roman Catholic Church in Portland, Maine,
of the clear blue lobster-water country . . . My

Grandfather's lawyer brother victim of what
seems to be a particular Irish disease, dark terrible
treachery; to the British against their own and

especially in families seeming to resent
another's success or owing them. My Grandfather
Michael The O'Dock's own brother for whom he

half-killed himself as a little boy to
work to earn enough money to buy a grocery store
for them all in America and send the money home so

his brothers could get off the boat educated men, his
lawyer brother cheated him and their mother so that
all my boyhood in Portland, Maine, of the clear blue

lobster-water country, there were "us" the State Street
O'Docks and across the city where my Grandfather
and his mother began in Portland, Maine, the Munjoy Hill

O'Docks never speaking, all my boyhood . . . I was
on strict orders never to ever say even "hello"
to a Munjoy Hill O'Dock . . . The Irish do each other

more harm than anyone could think up
to do to them, there's a savage self-destructiveness
in us, we want death . . . want to reminisce

longingly about what could have been . . . My Grandfather
The O'Dock ordered a house to be built of granite
in Portland, Maine, of the clear blue lobster-water country

O'Dock emblazoned into the front door
on a thick bronze nameplate of the house my
Grandfather Michael The O'Dock built and

on the edge of the curb of the sidewalk in
front of the house, a big granite stone to step
out onto from horse-drawn carriages and

later, cars. Sometimes through the years
I drive all the way to Portland, Maine, from
wherever I am and sit in my car in

front of bleak redbrick Saint Dominic's,
furious in the stench of incense, across
the street from the house my Grandfather built

for us all, but times change and money's value.
We O'Docks though proud were dumb to the
real world, frightened by the Irish screaming faith,

beaten into us, eliminating us as competition.
We were submissives though it is a
treacherous mean low thing to say about your own.

My Grandfather's only son Big Billy spent his
life fantasizing himself as everything he wasn't
and would like to have been—a "Broadway

Dapper Dandy," "Fred Astaire," yet he wasn't ignorant.

The church and a spoiled bringing-up had him on
his knees. He was an educated man who
needed approval, to get back for what he suspected

he could never dare to put his finger on—had been
robbed from him, instilled with guilts, never
daring to make a move without getting down on his knees

and blessing himself and reciting endless
words called prayers in fear if he didn't
"God" would "strike him dead" . . . an educated man

who studied kitchen-Greek under John Alden, yes,
a descendant of who you think and liked to believe
he could kitchen-Greek with shoeshine parlor Greeks who,

in the problem of social climbing from one position to
another, were tickled, flattered that a man of the
fair-colored skin of the ruling Wasp with blue eyes, too, would

"tryna garble" whatever it was he tried to garble
with them from his Greek studies. They were all really
hustling together in this new land of opportunity

where money expresses how royal you are . . . Big Billy
used to be so frustrated, held back, restrained from
bursting forth, the real Big Billy! by two

children left him by a dead mother . . . Big Billy
used to scream, "God will strike you dead!"
to us, but he had a style and a smile for every adult.
He was afraid of grown-ups, only tough with weak

and helpless children, or people who worked for him . . . he
forgot children grow up and remember . . . Then he'd
"feel bad." Big Billy would feel bad

and meet you after school go buy you an ice cream
sundae which better make it alright! better
make everything alright! His seething fury threat

waited for you not to accept
an ice cream all right! But he was a
good man according to his lights. He needed

the Irish church permission but he was a
good man, the best of the broken Irish
descended from a man of futile courage

who stumbled here to America, his hand clutched
in his mother's from God's empty potato fields
and said goodbye forever to County Clare . . . Clare

of wild violet Irish Atlantic like the
clear blue lobster-water country, fresh in salt,
the wind screaming your heart's lust joy in its whistle

and down deep the lobsters crawling oblivious as
all God's good creatures about their murders as if
no one knows and they are ordained for it, so,

when we sink our traps, it is our killing . . . it was
only little children Big Billy raged at, raged his
own bitter disappointments on, biting

a handkerchief and screaming until
his face burst bloodred frothing spittle
rolling down his chin because he couldn't

muster himself for himself, and after all,
children always have been perfect victims, like
cats, small, not able to fight back against

"God will strike you dead" and "I must be appeased!"
Children "t'be seen-n-not heard-n-y'didn't
have a right to an opinion until y'30!"

XIX

Perhaps Big Billy secretly knew underneath his terror
that God wouldn't really strike you dead for
thinking for yourself, but too late that "God"

wouldn't "strike you dead" for being open-minded
and living this life He put you in trying
to imagine how to step on the Moon . . . Big Billy

somehow had been cheated, he sensed, but he couldn't
touch exactly what had been done to him and by whom,
certainly not by his lovely adoring wonderful mother,

not by The O'Dock, that he could see! Th-at he could see!!
Frothing red-faced in his spittle screech, his rage caught
in his handkerchief biting for the life robbed from him, he

could have been Damon Runyon!! . . . if he hadn't been made
to feel he better get right down on his knees praying
and asking God forgiveness, not out there, out competing,

out fighting for a piece of Protestantland . . . so, frustrated,
worse, not ever knowing why he was so angry he forced
his own children to loathe him for his screech

in sardine stench, all the petals

of wildflowers flew off their
stems in his bellow . . .

XX

. . . Oh and many an Irish immigrant youth
cursed by Saint Patrick myth and
stupidity, foolish pride bragging how

they were able to succeed enough to spare
their children what they had to do, and in
doing this, making many an Irish-American youth

as crippled as he is back home in
the rough green Irish Sea country but in
Ireland it's more from sheer futility

at lack of any opportunity to use your
talent through judgmental suppression into
the child in America where the Irish

fled to prosper from black potato core
the children of the immigrant's children
unable to speak for themselves, asking others

in the Protestant competition to put in
a good word for them while cold rain slammed
the window of warm house inside which

they were comfy cuddled right out of their lives in
Mother's cold next-day meat pies never getting
started, not able to go out and make themselves

stand up on their own two feet and open their own mouths
and come right out and ask, ask! . . . even for
a sewer job . . . so ended American promise

in Michael The O'Dock . . . so ended the chance taking, the
beautiful riskers that are the greatness of a country,
ended the functioning that must come from

inside us in each and every one of us, promise
gone as much to the bottle here in America
as any Irish farmer with Ireland,

green Ireland, violent Ireland grape in its yearning,
Ireland always green in his eyes but alcohol
his early death with all the old boys crying

for The O'Dock who sailed away, his hand clutched
in his mother's forever from Ireland, Eire
of my soul my flesh wanders the earth . . .

XXI

Oh, my Grandfather The O'Dock ordered a house
to be built of granite right across the street from
God's house, Saint Dominic's Church in Portland,

Maine, of the clear blue lobster-water country. Truly
this granite house was Irish success in America.
But after the last daughter of Michael The O'Dock, my

Grandfather, died at 91 the house was sold, the
house that Michael The O'Dock came over to
America, as a little boy with his hand clutched

in his mother's, to rush from and survive
potato famine and earn enough to bring his
two brothers over just as soon as they could; all

the life's work, sweat of The O'Dock was just sold!

I, Bop, was unable to keep it . . . (didn't have any money)
(smell your own orifices) the house had no money

to keep itself. We were all poor from beating
our breasts in Mea Culpa instead of going out
into American opportunity with our lies and kiting checks

anything to keep our Grandfather's house. Anything!
We went our separate ways, Young Billy
so glad to escape me, to get away from the

stifling death in my aunt's and the suspicion
that all Bop, me, Bop wanted was to steal
money out of his wallet while he lay asleep in bed

in our Grandfather's granite house . . .
. . . He once told me he was watching me like a mouse,
meaning it too, he wasn't free of that house, those people,

Big Billy . . . and I had to rush away too, so looked like
a young bum running who would need support and Young Billy
wasn't going to give me any, I was on my own!

We are a damned breed, the Irish. Young Billy gave
his whole identity to Big Billy just to try
to have his love . . .

destruction of ourselves by ourselves
until we are all forgotten
dead among the dead . . .

XXII

. . . Throughout my manhood, throughout the

years, I often drive all the way back to
Portland, Maine, and sit in my car across

the street from the house I spent half my
boyhood in, I often go just to sit across the
street in my car to at least see the house my

Grandfather, Michael The O'Dock, built after coming
all the way from County Clare, Ireland, with
nothing a'tall. There were statements

in Help Wanted "No Irish need apply"
for the idea of America sold to the lowest
common man was that we would all be able to

worship God any way we wanted and beJesus-
screeching Irish Priests or Roman Catholic
worshipers were suspect of planning to

take over United States Constitution
just as soon as they could get enough
brush and firewood to start burning

people alive again who wouldn't take
the Wafer and the Mea Culpa . . . Often I
sit in my car in front of Saint Dominic's

Roman Catholic Church in Portland, Maine, of the
clear blue lobster-water country knowing someone
else has my home, but does not realize it, good

people, I'm sure, who must sense
a broken heart sitting across the street
in a car still in the scent of incense, but

they never open the door
or peer out so I sit
until I cannot.

XXIII

Here living in among other
immigrants of Protestant New England,
it was better to clip and harden your name

to make it easy for other people who,
after all, would be your customers as well as
neighbors, people who weren't Irish to say

your name easily, not be annoyed and go buy
bread and milk some place easy to say the
owner's name, so my Grandfather dropped the O

and became bluntly Mike Dock easy to
say, to hear, to deal with, not
aggravating, not anybody thinking

you were putting on airs in this
new country using some
fancy-sounding name like

"O'Dock" which was your name, but
not here, not in the Protestant
New England clear blue

lobster-water country, not here where
you've come just to eat, to stay alive
away from where potatoes wouldn't grow

where potatoes wouldn't
grow even if Jesus
asked them to Himself.

XXIV

In the old country, the Irish
would put on the headstones of
the graves left forever, the names

of Michael The O'Dock and his mother's
and his brothers' names on their
nearest relatives' gravestones, their

names and the dates they died
in America . . . and in America too
O'Dock went on my Grandfather's

own gravestone, but none of his children
even had identity enough in their
own minds to insist on their

names on headstones, there
are no names on the graves or
even stones over the graves of Michael

The O'Dock's children in America,
almost as if each and every one of them
felt he had never really wanted them.

His dong worked for the church
so he'd done his duty and could go
to Heaven, rather than wanting his

own children, no, they have no grave stones

but lie under the earth purchased for
them by their father doing what he

felt he had to do like wiping his ass
to be in good with Jesus, ravaging
his wife for a son until he got one

again and again, furiously, frantically
dong rape of the
mother of his twelve girls, girls don't count!

He wept, it was a family story that
he sat down on the steps of his granite house
and cried when he got the news that

after twelve girls he had Big Billy.
His girls now lie in the land he bought them
in the earth papa provided for them, as if

they never felt they had a right to purchase
their own forever place, as if they never felt
they had a right to put a stone

over themselves with their individual
names on it—No one can find them
and few are looking for them or ever will

or will ever visit them, even on Memorial Day.
They lived and died as if they'd never been
in America—in the clear blue lobster-water country

and the very name O'Dock, "Dock" lost vanishing
on His, The O'Dock's gravestone but what
planned revenge on him by his own girls, they

would never buy their own graves, their own earth
but lie in what he bought them with no
headstones over themselves, since he had never

wanted them or even picked them up when
they were little, to sit on his knee and be told
he loved them by him, so, after a lifetime of

consciously forever smelling their own orifices,
themselves as foul unwanted, they vanished forever
without a trace except in city and state and church

records in the clear blue lobster-water country
and the very name O'Dock lost—on Michael
The O'Dock's gravestone, but abbreviated in

his daily doings to make it easier to do business.
Yes, the name "O'Dock" is on Big Billy's gravestone,
Yes, it will be on Young Billy's and on mine too.

But the absence of it and the lack of gravestones for
any of Michael The O'Dock's daughters is that final unseen
unimagined failure that can come to us

who work so hard but inside ourselves, not
ever letting anyone we love know
we love them; it would bewilder us

that they would think we didn't, our
frustrated rage at being trapped by our income
let loose in silent resentment that is loud

in our house, misinterpreted,
our children thought we didn't want them . . .
while you yell that no man will ever

make you tip your forelock but doing it while
you're saying you're not and then feeling terrible
taking it out on your own children, so your soul

purpose is gone in the new land too . . . robbed
of our individuality by never hearing or
feeling our Father ever loved us, by the

browbeating tip-your-forelock
Roman Church, tricked out of life on
this earth for the next . . . "Dock" into the front door

of his granite house oh, it was
quite elegant for a self-made man to have!
From Ireland to America! Right across

the street from his parish
church, gone from the Docks in
less than sixty years . . .

XXV

. . . Father, it is night . . . see the
clear silk black death hovering to
enfold me . . . But I am not quite ready.

No one is ever going to be ready, we love to
think of an eternity in which we are finally happy
and it is always assumed that of course we'd

want to be with Mom and Dad and all our relatives
and old friends, when, perhaps, eternal
happiness is really oblivion, solitude in which

to contemplate and finally the answer as to the

"reason for everything," life, death, murder,
sorrow, torture, pain, why what was . . .

Father I'd
like to be the Apple Cheek kid
whose picture you

carried in your wallet
once more
oh, Father, once more!

I
love you still . . . I remember
the smell of the sweat of you

in the old shirt you always left
on a hanger with a pair
of knickers, old clothes

to put on when you came to
the cottage in Old Orchard Beach, Maine,
of the clear blue lobster-water country.

I'd hug it to my nose in my loneliness
left at the beach where you thought a little boy
would want to be—but I wanted to be with you.

—but I was the kid who
reminded you too much of Mother . . . your
sister, my aunt, one of Michael The O'Dock's daughters

would say to me, when she noticed my need for you,
Father . . . how I mustn't mind if it seemed
you couldn't ever look straight at me much, I

reminded you so much of Mother that my aunt, your sister,
one of Michael The O'Dock's girls, said to me was why, I
looked so much like my mother you couldn't bear it; just

what was I supposed to do about it, vanish!? How should I
feel being told that I looked like the mother who had
to go somewhere and you could hardly stand looking

at me, I reminded you of her so much, when that
wasn't it!? You know and I know, from the times I've
wished I zipped up, Father, it could be every time

you saw me, had to look at me, knowing your Jesus-knit-browed Jesus
was probably gonna burn you in Hellfire forever and forever,
and, see how clever He is, part of your punishment right here

on earth before you get to leave to burn forever is having
to look at me, at what you did for which
God-ud strike you dead, it was never that

you were gonna go whether you were Arab,
Protestant, Jewish, no, it was me, me that
created your Hell, you did it but I was it . . .

We have killed our own seed in its ground.
But I slipped out in time, Mother,
I myself escaped.

XXVI

Big Billy lies buried in Thomaston, Maine, of
the clear blue lobster-water country, under a
headstone he bought economically. Already

the tombstone in just brief years since

Big Billy fell and hit that great bald head
to death on garage oil-stained concrete,

the tombstone is falling over with both Big Billy's
name and our mother's, names deeply embedded
as if once the stone was soft and their

names deep cut-in like by a cookie design, their
carved names are now filled with fungus green
although Big Billy dutifully paid for "Perpetual Care";

he's hardly in the ground and all meaning of him's
going, of his famous rages and Mea Culpa . . .
But in American Depression in which one was lucky

to have a plate of beans, especially with
fat slipping in among them, you
bought the surest thing you could so you'd

have it! The Economy Headstone even if
it did mean having your name and birth
date carved on it with the date of your own

death blank for you to have to see as the
weary years went by as you visited with
your two boys Bop and Young Billy the place

you told them, when you went there on her
birth date and your Wedding anniversary,
was where Mamma was but it was confusing and

you didn't dare ever ask, for fear Big Billy's
face would suddenly fill as if he was going
to blow a horn and turn beet red

before from deep within
him rage burst forth
an "I must be appeased!"

. . . Wasn't Mamma away taking care of a
little boy who needed her more than they did?
How come!? How come then we come to this place

a graveyard every time it's her birth date
or the two of you's Weddin' anniversary and
you tell us she's there in the earth

before taking us boys out for a special dinner
and after maybe a movie like we do on our own
birthdays, so we'll always think of Momma

as always being with us? . . . How can she be away
taking care of a little boy who needs her more
than we do . . . and at the same time in this earth.

XXVII

—Already the tombstone Big Billy paid for up front
when Momma died is crumbling from neglect—
it used to irritate him to see his name

carved in it deep beside hers with the date of
his birth, blank, the date of his mortality (how
many times must he play with the date,

fill it in with despair!?) Big Billy never missing
Friday night Benediction and Stations Of The Cross once and
always going to early, early Mass,

Five O'Clock Mass, his whole individuality

given up to a warm sensual fright love of God
in terror of His striking him dead . . .

XXVIII

Big Billy lies buried now in Thomaston, Maine, of
the clear blue lobster-water country, beside our mother
who was crumbled dust before I was a grown man.

But she gave me myself and now I give myself to her.
How come in my secret head I'm thinking
all the time what I was told on a Christmas eve

when I was seven, that Mamma just went to be with
a little boy who needed her more than
I did, than me and Young Billy did, but, as

if that was never said never told me, by the
time I'm ten years old we go with Big Billy
not batting an eye out to the old meadow

the community put its dead into forever
and God help me if I'd ever bring it up
but my heart wanted to believe my Mamma'd

come back to me . . . but don't ever dare
bring it up to Big Billy, how can she be in
this earth you keep bringing us to and

away taking care of another little boy who
needed her more than I did, we did? Oh
I wanted her to be with

that other boy and maybe
maybe coming back sometime
then in this earth.

XXIX

A drop of testicle juice hit her egg
and here I am in love with her.
We never knew each other as adults

but I am, finally, what she made me,
cuddling me in her arms and walking
me when I was puny sick and all

the while whispering to me that she
loved me and if there was another
boy she went to who needed her

more than I did she never once
ever loved him like she loved my
brother Young Billy and me . . .

not for a split instant . . . so all you
grown-ups who didn't know how to
just let me share my grief in her dying

I rise above you, whatever you ever did to me,
I am put together again hard, I will break
no further, I have become me.

                    Down down deep in the sea
                    th'lobster wait for
                    Father's Lahty . . .

XXX

"Mr. Dock," accordion
jello face snapped Boppledock
back . . . "They're

here to lift you to hospital."
Weakly, very tired, Boppledock
wearily nodded . . .

"Hey, pal . . . you all right!?"
"Am I all right!! Wha-choo
talkin' 'bout?" Bop laughed . . .

. . . "Know what, Sergeant . . . I mean
Master Sergeant Alfred Kelly!?"
Accordion jello face dropped easily

to his haunches again beside
Bop like he'd pulled this kind
of duty since the beginning of time . . .

"What's funny, old fella?" Bop
looked up . . . the young guerrilla who
had pointed the automatic

at him when there was a threat
he would shake up life, had
appeared and stood now by

accordion jello face. Bop shook his head to
clear his vision, just for a split instant
accordion jello face's

features seemed to change

like seeing a skull through an X ray.
"Tell you somethin' " Bop seemed

almost shy . . . "I all of a sudden sure
don't feel like fightin' f'much." He
looked very hard at accordion

jello face. "I guess you don't
see what I mean" . . . the young
guerrilla reached a pack of

cigarettes over to Bop . . . "No, they're
death!" Bop shuddered. Master Sergeant
Kelly looked at the young guerrilla

like a boss at a subordinate. "I see
what you mean." Accordion
jello face whispered.

"Y'know," Bop went on as if
he hadn't heard him . . . "Kelly, d'you know
if you could ever git to th'point

where you can do somethin'
with no profit in it f'you . . ."
Accordion jello face's head was nodding.

A breeze blew the birthday candles out of
Bop's eyes . . . The old Victrola
was broken and the needle of Bop going

aimlessly all over the record . . . Accordion
jello face stood up. It was apparent
he was no longer needed . . .

. . . "Don't worry,"
he said grinning . . .
"The world won't end, it's too expensive!"

Lying on the stretcher Bop watched
the young guerrilla holding a piece of
polished tin he was using as a mirror

slanting bright bright sun at Bop as he was
entranced with the joy of his young image.
Bop's eyes winced shut against that

bright flash imprinted on his lids, dark
boxes vibrating like heartbeats
trying to thrust through and floating

through Bop's thoughts; I've progressed
in th'possibility of annihilation with
th'knowledge that like a young guerrilla

controlling th'sun in a piece of tin
we all must see to it th'sun doesn't
get away from us . . . Bop thought now

of Mercutio's wound, a strange gladness in
the remembrance. He hugged these thoughts
like a fine companion met again

in this new place. Feeling himself
lifted now, Bop
closed his eyes.

THE END